"More is a man of an angel's wit and singular learning; I know not his fellow. For where is the man of that gentleness, lowliness and affability? And as time requireth a man of marvellous mirth and pastimes; and sometimes of as sad gravity: a man for all seasons."

ROBERT WHITTINTON

"He was the person of the greatest virtue these islands ever produced."

SAMUEL JOHNSON

A MAN FOR ALL SEASONS

Produced by H. M. Tennent Ltd at the Globe Theatre, London, on the 1st July 1960, with the following cast of characters:

(in the order of their appearance)

THE COMMON MAN	*Leo McKern*
SIR THOMAS MORE	*Paul Scofield*
MASTER RICHARD RICH	*John Bown*
THE DUKE OF NORFOLK, Earl Marshal of England	*Alexander Gauge*
LADY ALICE MORE, Sir Thomas's wife	*Wynne Clark*
LADY MARGARET MORE, Sir Thomas's daughter	*Pat Keen*
CARDINAL WOLSEY	*Willoughby Goddard*
THOMAS CROMWELL	*Andrew Keir*
SIGNOR CHAPUYS, the Spanish Ambassador	*Geoffrey Dunn*
CHAPUYS' ATTENDANT	*Brian Harrison*
WILLIAM ROPER	*John Carson*
KING HENRY THE EIGHTH	*Richard Leech*
A WOMAN	*Beryl Andrews*
THOMAS CRANMER, Archbishop of Canterbury	*William Roderick*

Directed by NOEL WILLMAN

Scenery and Costumes by MOTLEY

SYNOPSIS OF SCENES

ACT I

ACT II

Time—the Sixteenth Century

SYNOPSIS OF SCENES

ACT I

Scene 1. Sir Thomas More's House at Chelsea
Scene 2. Wolsey's apartment at Richmond
Scene 3. The grounds at Richmond
Scene 4. Sir Thomas More's House
Scene 5. Hampton Court Palace
Scene 6. The garden of Sir Thomas More's house
Scene 7. An Inn

ACT II

Scene 1. Sir Thomas More's house
Scene 2. Cromwell's apartment at Hampton Court
Scene 3. Sir Thomas More's house
Scene 4. Cromwell's apartment at Hampton Court
Scene 5. The riverside at Hampton Court
Scene 6. The Tower of London
Scene 7. The same
Scene 8. The Hall of Westminster
Scene 9. Tower Hill

Time—the Sixteenth Century

ACT I

SCENE—*The main setting is the same throughout, but is varied by lighting
and the addition of scenic items to indicate the venue of the action. A lightly
constructed curved stairway from a rostrum up R, leads up and off L. From
the rostrum, four steps lead to ground level RC. On the rostrum, at the foot
of the stairway, there is a slender pillar reaching up to the flies. The stairway has a light hand-rail on the upstage side, and the top is masked at the
downstage side by a light window grille. Black wings mask the setting R
and L and a cyclorama fills the background. At the opening of the Play,
there is a refectory table C, with a large armchair L of it and a small chair
R of it. There is a short bench below the rostrum R, and a small stool is in
the curve of the stairway RC. A large property basket stands down L.*
Before the CURTAIN *rises, a loud, single bell rings.*

When the CURTAIN *rises, the setting is in darkness. The bell stops. A single
spot comes on, focused vertically on* THE COMMON MAN *who is seated on
the basket. He is in late middle age. He wears from head to foot, black
tights which delineate his pot-bellied figure. His face is crafty, loosely
benevolent, its best expression that of base humour.*

COMMON MAN. It is perverse! To start a play made up of Kings
and Cardinals in speaking costumes and intellectuals with em-
broidered mouths, with me. If a King or Cardinal had done the
Prologue he'd have had the right materials. And an intellectual
would have shown enough majestic meanings, coloured propositions,
and closely woven liturgical stuff to dress the House of Lords. (*He
rises to show off his costume*) But this! Is this a costume? Does this say
anything? It barely covers one man's nakedness. A bit of black
material to reduce Old Adam to the Common Man. (*He moves
forward a step or two*) Oh, if they'd let me come on naked, I could have
shown you something of my own. Which would have told you without words—something I've forgotten—Old Adam's muffled up. (*He
backs to the basket*) Well, for a proposition of my own, I need a costume
(*He takes the coat and hat of a Steward from the basket and puts them on*)
Matthew!   **Scene 1**

(*The general lighting comes up*)

The Household Steward of Sir Thomas More. (*He takes from the
basket a wicker tray on which there are five goblets, a silver cup and a pewter
jug of wine with a lid*)

(*A burst of conversational merriment is heard off up* L)

(*He indicates the head of the stairway*) There's company to dinner.
(*He puts the jug, cup and goblets on the left end of the table*) All right! A

Common Man! A Sixteenth-Century Butler! (*He drinks from the jug*)
All right—the Six—(*He breaks off, agreeably surprised by the quality of
the liquor, regards the jug respectfully and drinks again*) The Sixteenth
Century is the Century of the Common Man. (*He replaces the tray
in the basket, closes it and pushes it to the side*) Like all the other centuries.
(*He pulls the chair* L *of the table below the left end of it, then crosses to* R *of
the stairway*) And that's my proposition.

(SIR THOMAS MORE *enters at the top of the stairway. He is in his late
forties. He is pale, middle-sized and not robust. But the life of the mind
in him is so abundant and debonair that it illuminates the body. His move-
ments are open and swift but never wild, having a natural moderation. The
face is intellectual and quickly delighted, the norm to which it returns serious
and compassionate. Only in moments of high crisis does it become ascetic,
though then freezingly*)

STEWARD. That's Sir Thomas More.
MORE (*descending the stairway*) The wine, please, Matthew.
STEWARD. It's there, Sir Thomas.
MORE (*crossing to* L *of the table*) Is it good?
STEWARD. Bless you, sir—*I* don't know.
MORE (*mildly*) Bless you, too, Matthew.

(MASTER RICHARD RICH *enters at the top of the stairway. He is in
his early thirties, and has a good body, unexercised. He has a studious,
unhappy face lit by the fire of banked down appetite. He is an academic
hounded by self-doubt to be in the world of affairs and longing to be rescued
from himself*)

RICH (*as he slowly descends the stairway; enthusiastically pursuing an
argument*) But every man has his price.
MORE. No, no!
STEWARD (*contemptuously*) Master Richard Rich.
RICH. But, yes! In money, too.
MORE (*with gentle impatience*) No, no, no! (*He pours wine*)
RICH. Or pleasure. Titles, women, bricks and mortar, there's
always something. (*He reaches the foot of the stairway*)
MORE. Childish.
RICH (*moving below the right end of the table*) Well, in suffering,
certainly.
MORE (*interested*) Buy a man with suffering?
RICH. Impose suffering, and offer him—escape.
MORE. Oh. For a moment I thought you were being profound.
(*He hands Rich a goblet of wine*)
RICH (*to the Steward*) Good evening, Matthew.
STEWARD (*snubbing*) 'Evening, sir.
RICH. No, not a bit profound; it then becomes a purely practical
question of how to make him suffer sufficiently.
MORE. M'm. (*He takes Rich by the arm and walks with him down* C)
And—who recommended you to read Signor Machiavelli?

(RICH *breaks away laughing; a fraction too long*)

(*He smiles*) No, who?

(RICH *laughs*)

Mm?

RICH. Master Cromwell.

MORE. Oh. (*He moves to the table*) He's a very able man.

RICH. And so he is!

MORE. Yes, I say he is. He's very able.

RICH (*moving up* C) And he will do something for me, he says.

MORE. I didn't know you knew him.

RICH (*moving above the right end of the table*) Pardon me, Sir Thomas, but how much do you know about me?

MORE. Whatever you've let me know.

RICH. I've let you know everything.

MORE. Richard, you should go back to Cambridge; you're deteriorating.

RICH. Well, I'm not used! D'you know how much I have to show for seven months' work . . . ?

MORE. Work?

RICH. Work! Waiting's work when you wait as I wait, hard! For seven months, that's two hundred days, I have to show: the acquaintance of the Cardinal's outer doorman, the indifference of the Cardinal's inner doorman, and the Cardinal's chamberlain's hand in my chest. Oh—also one half of a "Good morning" delivered at fifty paces by the Duke of Norfolk. Doubtless he mistook me for someone.

MORE. He was very affable at dinner.

RICH. Oh, everyone's affable *here*.

(MORE *is pleased*)

Also, of course, the friendship of Sir Thomas More. Or should I say "acquaintance"?

MORE. Say "friendship".

RICH. Well, there! "A friend of Sir Thomas" and still no office? There must be something wrong with him.

MORE. I thought we said "friendship". (*He considers*) The Dean of St Paul's offers you a post; with a house, a servant, and fifty pounds a year.

RICH. What? What post?

MORE. At the new school.

RICH (*bitterly disappointed*) A teacher! (*He moves to* L *of the steps*)

MORE. A man should go where he won't be tempted. (*He picks up the silver cup and crosses to* L *of Rich*) Look, Richard, see this. (*He hands the cup to Rich*) Look. Look.

RICH. Beautiful.

MORE. Italian. Do you want it?

RICH. Why . . . ?

MORE. No joke; keep it; or sell it.

RICH. Well, I . . . Thank you, of course—thank you. Thank you.
But . . . ?

MORE. You'll sell it, won't you?

RICH. Well, I . . . Yes, I will.

MORE.. And buy, what?

RICH (*with sudden ferocity*) Some decent clothes.

MORE (*with sympathy*) Ah!

RICH. I want a gown like yours.

MORE. You'll get several gowns for that, I should think. It was
sent to me a little while ago by some woman. Now she's put a law-
suit into the Court of Requests. It's a bribe, Richard.

RICH. Oh. (*Chagrined*) So you give it away, of course.

MORE. Yes.

RICH. To me.

MORE. Well, I'm not going to keep it, and you need it. Of course,
if you feel it's contaminated . . .

RICH. No, no. I'll risk it.

(*They both smile.* RICH *moves to* R *of the table and puts the cup on it*)

MORE (*moving to the armchair* LC *and sitting*) But, Richard, in office
they offer you all sorts of things. I was once offered a whole village,
with a mill, and a manor house, and Heaven knows what else—a
coat of arms, I shouldn't be surprised. Why not be a teacher? You'd
be a fine teacher. Perhaps—a great one.

RICH. And if I was who would know it?

MORE. You, your pupils, your friends. God—not a bad public,
that. Oh, and a *quiet* life.

RICH (*laughing*) *You* say that!

MORE. Richard, I was commanded into office; it was inflicted on
me.

(RICH *regards More*)

Can't you believe that?

RICH. It's hard. (*He moves above the table*)

MORE (*grimly*) Be a teacher.

NORFOLK (*off*) It was magnificent!

(*The* DUKE OF NORFOLK, *Earl Marshal of England, enters at the top
of the stairway. He is in his late forties. He is heavy, active, a sportsman
and soldier held together by rigid adherence to the minimal code of con-
ventional duty. Attractively aware of his moral and intellectual insignifi-
cance, but also a great nobleman, untouchably convinced that his acts and
ideas are important because they are his. He comes into view and stops,
looking back.* MORE *rises and moves to* L *of the table*)

STEWARD (*to the audience*) The Duke of Norfolk. Earl Marshal of
England.

NORFOLK (*looking off* L) I tell you he stooped from the clouds . . . (*He breaks off. Irritably*) Alice!

(LADY ALICE *enters at the top of the stairway. She is in her late forties. Born into the merchant class, now a great lady, she is absurd at a distance, impressive close to. Overdressed, coarsely fashioned, she worships society; brave, hot-hearted, she worships her husband. In consequence, troubled by and defiant towards both*)

ALICE (*irritably*) Here!
STEWARD (*to the audience*) Lady Alice. My master's wife.
NORFOLK. I tell you he stooped . . .
ALICE (*crossing below Norfolk and descending the stairway*) He didn't!

(MARGARET MORE *enters at the top of the stairway. She is in her middle twenties. She is a beautiful girl of ardent moral fineness. She both suffers and shelters behind a reserved stillness which it is her father's care to mitigate*)

NORFOLK (*following Alice down the stairway*) Goddammit, he did!
ALICE. Couldn't!
NORFOLK. He *does*.
ALICE. Not possible!
ALICE (*moving down* C) Never!
NORFOLK (*moving to* R *of the table*) Well, damn my soul!
MORE (*to Margaret*) Come down, Meg.
STEWARD (*to the audience; soapy*) Lady Margaret, my master's daughter—lovely, really lovely.
ALICE. Matthew, get about your business.

(*The* STEWARD *exits down* R. MARGARET *descends the stairway*)

(*She moves below the table*) We'll settle this, my lord. We'll put it to Thomas. Thomas, no falcon could stoop from a cloud, could it?
MORE. I don't know, my dear; it sounds unlikely. I have seen falcons do some very splendid things.
ALICE. But how could he stoop from a cloud? He couldn't see where he was going. (*She sits in the armchair* LC)

(MORE *pours wine for Alice and Norfolk*)

NORFOLK. You see, Alice—you're ignorant of the subject: a falcon like Hector don't *care* where he's going.

(MORE *hands a goblet to Norfolk*)

Thank you, Thomas. (*He turns to Margaret*) Anyway, I'm talking to Meg.

(MORE *moves to* L *of the table, hands a goblet to Alice, then pours wine for Margaret and himself*)

(*He resumes his "sportsman's" story*) 'Twas the very first cast of the day, Meg; the sun was behind us. And from side to side of the valley like the roof of a tent, was solid mist.

ALICE. Oh—mist.

NORFOLK. Well, mist is cloud, isn't it?

ALICE. No.

RICH (*with a step down stage*) The opinion of Aristotle is that mists are an exhalation of the earth whereas clouds . . .

NORFOLK. He stooped five hundred feet! Like *that!* Like an act of God, isn't he, Thomas?

MORE. He's tremendous.

NORFOLK (*to Alice*) Tremendous.

MARGARET. Did he kill the heron?

NORFOLK. Oh, the *heron.* The heron was *clever.* (*Very discreditable, evidently*) It was a royal stoop, though. (*Slyly*) If you could ride, Alice, I'd show you. (*He moves below the table and sits on the downstage edge of it*)

ALICE (*hotly*) I can ride, my lord!

MORE. No, no, you'll make yourself ill. (*He takes a goblet to Margaret and gives it to her*)

ALICE. And I'll bet—twenty-five—no, thirty shillings I see no falcon stoop from no cloud.

NORFOLK. Done!

MORE. Alice—you can't ride with *them.*

ALICE. God's body, Thomas, remember who you are. Am I a City Wife?

MORE. No, indeed. You've just lost thirty shillings, I think; there *are* such birds. (*To Margaret, gently teasing*) And the heron got home to his chicks, Meg, so everything was satisfactory. (*He gets his own goblet and sits R of the table*)

MARGARET (*smiling*) Yes.

MORE. What was that of Aristotle's, Richard?

RICH (*moving down L of the table*) Nothing, Sir Thomas—'twas out of place.

NORFOLK (*to Rich*) I've never found much use in Aristotle, myself —not practically. Great philosophy, of course. Wonderful mind.

RICH (*crossing to L of Norfolk*) Exactly, Your Grace.

NORFOLK (*suspiciously*) Eh?

MORE. Master Rich is newly converted to the doctrines of Machiavelli.

RICH. Oh, no . . .

NORFOLK. Oh, the Italian. Nasty book, from what I hear.

MARGARET (*moving to the foot of the steps*) Very practical, Your Grace.

NORFOLK. You read it? Amazing girl, Thomas, but where are you going to find a husband for her?

(MORE *and* MARGARET *exchange a glance*)

MORE. Where indeed?

(MARGARET *moves to* R *of More and holds his hand for a moment*)

RICH (*crossing down* L) The doctrines of Machiavelli have been largely mistake, I think; indeed, properly apprehended he has no doctrine. Master Cromwell has the sense of it, I think, when he says . . .

NORFOLK. You know Cromwell?

(MARGARET *moves up* C)

RICH. Slightly, Your Grace.

NORFOLK. The Cardinal's secretary.

(*There are exclamations of shock from* MORE, MARGARET *and* ALICE)

It's a fact. .

MORE (*rising, crossing and standing below the steps*) When, Howard?

(MARGARET *moves to* L *of More*)

NORFOLK. Two, three days.

ALICE (*rising and moving to* L *of the table*) A *farrier's* son?

NORFOLK. Well, the Cardinal's a butcher's son, isn't he?

ALICE. It'll be up quick and down quick with Master Cromwell.

(NORFOLK *grunts*)

MORE (*with a step down* RC; *to Rich, quietly*) Did you know this?

RICH. No!

MARGARET (*moving between More and Norfolk*) Do you *like* Master Cromwell, Master Rich?

ALICE. He's the only man in London if he does.

RICH. I think I do, Lady Alice.

(*The* STEWARD *enters* R, *crosses to* R *of More and hands him a letter*)

MORE (*pleased*) Good! Well, you don't need *my* help now. (*He opens the letter and reads it*)

RICH. Sir Thomas, if only you knew how much, much rather I'd yours than his.

MORE. Talk of the Cardinal's secretary and the Cardinal appears. He wants me. Now.

(*There are smothered exclamations of impatience*)

ALICE. At this time of night?

MORE (*mildly*) The King's business.

ALICE. The Queen's business.

NORFOLK (*rising and moving above the table*) More than likely, Alice, more than likely.

MORE (*cutting in sharply; to the Steward*) What's the time?

STEWARD. Eleven o'clock, sir.

MORE. Is there a boat?

STEWARD. Waiting, sir. (*He moves up* R)

MORE (*crossing to* C; *to Alice and Margaret*) Go to bed. You'll excuse me, Your Grace? Richard?

(ALICE *moves to* L *of More and* MARGARET *to* R *of him*)

(*To Alice and Margaret*) Now you'll go to bed.

(MORE, ALICE *and* MARGARET, *as a matter of routine, put their hands together. The* STEWARD *removes his hat. During the prayer,* NORFOLK *refills his goblet and drinks*)

ALICE ⎫
MORE ⎬ (*together*) ⎰ Dear Lord, give us rest tonight, or if we
MARGARET ⎭   ⎱ must be wakeful, cheerful. Careful only for our souls' salvation. For Christ's sake. Amen.

MORE. And bless our Lord the King.

ALICE ⎫
MARGARET ⎬ (*together*) And bless our Lord the King.

ALL. Amen.

(ALICE *crosses and goes on to the bottom step of the stairway.* MARGARET *goes on to the rostrum and stands at the top of the steps.* NORFOLK *moves to the foot of the steps.* RICH *puts his goblet on the table then moves to* L *of More*)

MORE (*to Norfolk*) Howard, are *you* at Richmond?

NORFOLK. No, down the river.

MORE. Then good night.

(RICH *looks disconsolate*)

Oh, Your Grace, here's a young man desperate for employment. Something in the clerical line.

NORFOLK. Well, if you recommend him . . .

MORE. Oh, I don't recommend him; but I point him out. (*He crosses to* LC) He's at the *New Inn.* You could take him there.

NORFOLK (*going on to the rostrum*) All right, come on.

RICH (*crossing to the foot of the steps*) My Lord.

NORFOLK. We'll hawk at Hounslow, Alice.

ALICE. Wherever you like.

(NORFOLK *takes farewell of* ALICE *and* MARGARET)

RICH. Sir Thomas.

(MORE *turns to Rich*)

Thank you.

(ALICE *and* MARGARET *go up the stairway*)

MORE. Be a teacher.

(RICH *exits* R *on the rostrum*)

Oh—the ground's hard at Hounslow, Alice.

NORFOLK. Eh? (*He gives a delighted roar of laughter*) That's where the Cardinal crushed his bum.

(MORE, ALICE *and* NORFOLK *call* "*good night*" *ad lib.*
NORFOLK *exits* R *on the rostrum.*
ALICE *and* MARGARET, *laughing, exit at the top of the stairway.*
MORE *exits up* L, *but re-enters immediately and stands below the stairway*)

MORE (*calling softly*) Margaret!

(MARGARET *enters at the top of the stairway*)

MARGARET. Yes?

MORE. Go to bed.

(MARGARET *exits at the top of the stairway.*
MORE *exits up* L. *There is a brief pause.*
RICH *enters swiftly* R *on the rostrum, crosses to the table, picks up the silver cup and turns to go*)

STEWARD. Eh! (*He crosses to* R *of Rich and takes the cup from him*)

RICH. What . . . ? Oh. It's a gift, Matthew. Sir Thomas gave it to me. He gave it to me.

STEWARD (*returning the cup to Rich*) Very nice present, sir.

RICH (*going on to the rostrum*) Yes. Good night, Matthew.

STEWARD (*moving to the foot of the steps*) Sir Thomas has taken quite a fancy to you, sir.

RICH (*giving the Steward some coins*) Er, here . . .

STEWARD. Thank you, sir.

(RICH *exits* R *on the rostrum. The* STEWARD, *during the following speech, moves anti-clockwise around the table turning in the corners of the cloth. He then takes the table-cloth with the goblets and jug inside and puts it in the basket. When he removes the white linen cloth from the table, a velour cloth is ready set underneath. From the basket he takes a brass ink-well, 2 quills and Wolsey's portfolio with papers and documents in it. He puts these on the table at the left end, and sets the armchair* L *of the table*)

(*To the audience*) That one'll come to nothing. My master—Thomas More would give anything to anyone. Some say that's good and some say that's bad, but I say he can't help it—and that's bad—because some day someone's going to ask him for something that he wants to keep; and he'll be out of practice. (*He goes to the basket and closes it*)

(*The* LIGHTS *change for the following scene*)

There must be something that he wants to keep. That's only Common Sense.

(*The* STEWARD *exits down* L, *pushing the basket off in front of him. A Pope's crown, resting on a tasselled panel is lowered from the flies and hangs over the armchair* L *of the table.*   **Scene 2**
CARDINAL WOLSEY *enters* R. *He is old. A big decayed body in scarlet. An almost megalomaniac ambition unhappily matched by an excelling intellect, he now inhabits a lonely den of self-indulgence and contempt. He carries a lighted candle in a brass candlestick. He crosses to* L *of the table, sits, sets the candlestick on the table in front of him and immediately commences writing.*
MORE, *carrying a lighted candle in a brass candlestick, enters at the top of the stairway and comes slowly down*)

WOLSEY (*writing*) Where've you been? It's half past one.

(*A bell strikes one*)

MORE. One o'clock, Your Grace. I've been on the river. (*He puts the candlestick on the table and stands above it, waiting*)

(WOLSEY *writes in silence for some moments, then still writing, he pushes a paper across the table to More*)

WOLSEY. Since you seemed so violently opposed to the despatch for Rome, I thought you'd like to look it over.
MORE (*touched*) Thank you, Your Grace.
WOLSEY. Before it goes.
MORE (*smiling*) Your Grace is very kind. (*He picks up the paper*) Thank you. (*He reads the paper*)
WOLSEY (*still writing*) Well, what d'you think of it?
MORE. It seems very well phrased, Your Grace. (*He puts the paper on the table*)

(WOLSEY *permits himself a chuckle*)

WOLSEY. The devil it does! (*He sits back*) And apart from the style, Sir Thomas?
MORE. I think the Council should be told before that goes to Italy.
WOLSEY. Would you tell the Council? Yes, I believe you would. You're a constant regret to me, Thomas. If you could just see facts flat on, without that horrible moral squint; with just a little common sense, you could have been a statesman.
MORE (*after a brief pause*) Oh, Your Grace flatters me.
WOLSEY. Don't frivol. Thomas, are you going to help me?

(MORE *hesitates and looks away*)

MORE. If Your Grace will be specific.
WOLSEY. Ach, you're a plodder. Take you altogether, Thomas, your scholarship, your experience—what are you?

(*A single trumpet calls, distant, frosty and clear*)

(*He rises, crosses and goes on to the rostrum* R) Come here.

(More *joins* Wolsey *on the rostrum and both look off* R)

The King.

More. Yes.

Wolsey. Where has he been? D'you know?

More. I, Your Grace?

Wolsey. Oh, spare me your discretion. He's been to play in the mud again.

More (*coldly*) Indeed!

Wolsey. Indeed! Indeed! Are you going to oppose me?

(*The trumpet call is repeated*)

(*He visibly relaxes*) He's gone in. (*He motions More down the steps*)

(More *moves down* R)

(*He moves down to* R *of More*) All right, we'll plod. The King wants a son; what are you going to do about it?

More (*in a dry manner*) I'm very sure the King needs no advice from me on what to do about it.

Wolsey (*fiercely gripping More's shoulder*) Thomas, we're alone. I give you my word. There's no-one here.

More (*with mild surprise*) I didn't suppose there was, Your Grace.

Wolsey. Oh. (*He crosses and sits* L *of the table*) Sit down! (*He signs to More to sit* R *of the table*)

(More *unsuspectingly obeys and sits* R *of the table*)

(*Deliberately loud*) Do you favour a change of dynasty, Sir Thomas? D'you think two Tudors is sufficient?

More (*rising in horrified alarm*) For God's sake, Your Grace . . . !

Wolsey. Then the King needs a son; I repeat, what are you going to do about it?

More (*steadily*) I pray for it daily.

Wolsey (*staring at More; softly*) God's death, he means it. That thing out there's at least fertile, Thomas.

More. But she's not his wife.

Wolsey. No, Catherine's his wife and she's as barren as brick. Are you going to pray for a miracle?

More. There *are* precedents.

Wolsey. Yes. All right. Good. Pray. Pray by all means. But in addition to Prayer there is Effort. My effort's to secure a divorce. Have I your support or have I not?

More (*resuming his seat*) A dispensation was granted so that the King might marry Queen Catherine, for State reasons. Now we are to ask the Pope to—dispense with his dispensation, also for State reasons?

Wolsey. I don't *like* plodding, Thomas—don't make me plod longer than I have to. Well?

MORE. Then clearly all we have to do is approach His Holiness and ask him.

(*The pace becomes rapid*)

WOLSEY. I think we might influence His Holiness's answer.
MORE (*indicating the letter*) Like this?
WOLSEY. Like that and in other ways.
MORE. I've already expressed my opinion on this.
WOLSEY (*rising*) Then—good night.

(MORE *rises. He and* WOLSEY *regard one another for a few moments*)

(*He moves down* L) Oh, your conscience is your own affair; but you're a statesman. Do you *remember* the Yorkist Wars?
MORE. Very clearly.
WOLSEY. Let him die without an heir and we'll have them back again. (*He moves to the table and picks up More's candlestick*) Let him die without an heir and this "peace" you think so much of will go out like—(*he extinguishes More's candle*) that! (*He puts down the candlestick and moves to* L *of the table*) Very well, then England needs an heir; certain measures, perhaps regrettable, perhaps not—(*pompously*) there is much in the Church that *needs* reformation, Thomas.

(MORE *smiles*)

All right, regrettable. But necessary to get us an heir. Now explain how you as a Councillor of England can obstruct those measures for the sake of your own, private conscience.
MORE. Well—(*he moves above the table, picks up his candlestick and relights his candle from Wolsey's*) I believe, when statesmen forsake their own private conscience for the sake of their public duties—they lead their country by a short route to chaos. And we shall have my prayers to fall back on.
WOLSEY. You'd like that, wouldn't you? To govern the country by prayer.
MORE. Yes, I should.
WOLSEY (*sitting* L *of the table*) I'd like to be there when you try. Who *will* deal with all this—paper, after me? You? Tunstall? Suffolk?
MORE. Tunstall for me.
WOLSEY. Aye, but for the King. What about my Secretary— Master Cromwell?
MORE. Cromwell!
WOLSEY. You'd rather do it yourself?
MORE. Me rather than Cromwell.
WOLSEY. Then come down to earth—and until then, allow for an enemy, here.
MORE. As Your Grace pleases. (*He moves with his candlestick to the steps*)
WOLSEY. As God wills.

MORE (*ascending the stairway*) Perhaps, Your Grace.

WOLSEY (*rising and gathering his portfolio and papers together*) More! You should have been a cleric.

MORE (*half-way up the stairway; amused*) Like yourself, Your Grace?

(MORE *exits at the top of the stairway.*

WOLSEY *stares after him for a few moments, then picks up his candlestick and exits up* L. *The* LIGHTS *cross fade and the whole rear of the stage now patterns with webbed reflections thrown from brightly moonlit water, so that the structure is thrown into black relief. The Pope's crown is raised and an oar and a bundle of clothing are lowered from the flies down stage.*

The COMMON MAN *enters down* L, *unties the bundle and dons the coat and hat of the* BOATMAN. *He is illuminated by the vertical spot*)

(*Off in the distance; calling*) Boat! (*Nearer*) Boat!

(*The* LIGHTS *come up down stage for the Riverside scene*)   **Scene 3**

BOATMAN (*calling*) Here, sir!

MORE (*off*) A boatman, please!

BOATMAN. Boat here, sir. (*He seizes the oar*)

(MORE *enters down the stairway*)

MORE (*peering*) Boatman?

BOATMAN. Yes, sir. (*To the audience, indicating the oar*) A boatman.

MORE. Take me home.

BOATMAN (*pleasantly*) I was just going home myself, sir. (*He moves* LC)

MORE (*moving to* R *of the Boatman*) Then find me another boat.

BOATMAN. Bless you, sir—that's all right. (*Comfortably*) I expect you'll make it worth my while, sir.

(THOMAS CROMWELL *enters* L. *He is in his late thirties. He is subtle and serious; the face expressing not inner tension but the tremendous outgoing will of the Renaissance. A self-conceit that can cradle gross crimes in the name of effective action. In short, an intellectual bully*)

CROMWELL. Boatman, have you a licence?

BOATMAN (*turning*) Eh? Bless you, sir—yes; I've got a licence.

CROMWELL. Then you know that the fares are fixed. (*He crosses below the Boatman to* L *of More. With exaggerated pleasure*) Why, it's Sir Thomas.

MORE. Good morning, Mister Cromwell. You work very late.

CROMWELL. I'm on my way to the Cardinal. (*He expects an answer*)

MORE. Ah.

CROMWELL. You have just left him, I think.

MORE. Yes, I have.

CROMWELL. You left him—in his laughing mood, I hope?

MORE. On the whole, I would say—not. No, not laughing.
CROMWELL. Oh, I'm sorry. (*He backs below the Boatman to* L) I
am one of your multitudinous admirers, Sir Thomas. (*To the Boatman*) A penny ha'penny to Chelsea, Boatman.

(CROMWELL *exits down* L)

BOATMAN. The coming man, they say, sir.
MORE. Do they? Well, where's your boat?
BOATMAN. Just along the wharf, sir. (*He crosses below More to* RC)

(MORE *turns to follow the Boatman.*
SIGNOR CHAPUYS, *the Spanish Ambassador enters down* L.
His ATTENDANT *follows him on.* CHAPUYS *is in his sixties. He is
a professional diplomat and lay ecclesiastic dressed in black. Much on his
dignity, as man of the world, he, in fact, trots happily along a mental
footpath as narrow as a peasant's. The* ATTENDANT *is an apprentice
diplomat of good family*)

CHAPUYS. Sir Thomas More! (*He crosses to* L *of More*)

(*The* BOATMAN *sits on the bench* R *of the steps. The* ATTENDANT
stands LC)

MORE. Signor Chapuys? You're up very late, Your Excellency.
CHAPUYS (*significantly*) So is the Cardinal, Sir Thomas.
MORE (*closing up*) He sleeps very little.
CHAPUYS. You have just left him, I think.
MORE. You are correctly informed. As always.
CHAPUYS. I will not ask you the subject of your conversation . . .
(*He waits*)
MORE. No, of course not.
CHAPUYS. Sir Thomas, I will be plain with you—plain, that is,
so far as the diplomatic decencies permit. (*Loudly*) My master—
Charles, the King of Spain . . . (*He draws More down* L. *Discreetly*)
My master—Charles, the King of Spain feels himself concerned in
anything concerning his blood relation. He would feel himself in-
sulted by any insult offered to his father's sister. I refer, of course,
to Queen Catherine. (*He regards More keenly*) The King of Spain
would feel himself insulted by any insult offered to Queen Catherine.
MORE. His feeling would be very natural.
CHAPUYS (*consciously sly*) Sir Thomas, may I ask if you and the
Cardinal parted, how shall I say, amicably?
MORE. Amicably—yes.
CHAPUYS (*a shade indignant*) In agreement?
MORE. Amicably.
CHAPUYS (*warmly*) Say no more, Sir Thomas; I understand. (*He
backs* L)
MORE (*a shade worried*) I hope you do, Your Excellency.
CHAPUYS. You are a good man.

MORE. I don't see how you deduce that from what I've told you.
CHAPUYS (*holding up a hand*) A nod is as good as a wink to a blind
horse. I understand. You are a good man. *Dominus vobiscum.*

(CHAPUYS *turns and exits* L.
    The ATTENDANT *follows him off.* MORE *looks after them for a few
moments*)

MORE (*abstracted*) . . . *spiritu tuo* . . .
BOATMAN (*mournfully*) People seem to think boats stay afloat on
their own, sir, but they don't; they cost money.

(MORE *gazes abstractedly out front*)

(*He rises and crosses to* R *of More*) Take anchor rope, sir, you may
not believe me, for a little skiff like mine, but it's a penny a fathom.

(MORE *is still abstracted*)

And with a young wife, sir, as you know . . .
MORE (*crossing below the Boatman to* R; *abstracted*) I'll pay what I
always pay you. The river looks very black tonight. They say it's
silting up—is that so?
BOATMAN (*moving to* L *of More*) Not in the middle, sir. There's a
channel there getting deeper all the time.
MORE. How *is* your wife?
BOATMAN. She's losing her shape, sir, losing it fast.
MORE. Well, so are we all.
BOATMAN. Oh, yes, sir; it's common.
MORE. Well, take me home.
BOATMAN. That I will, sir.

(MORE *exits down* R. *The front lighting and the ripple effect fade,
leaving only the vertical spot. During the following speech the* COMMON
MAN *crosses, exits* L *with the oar and re-enters immediately, pulling on
the basket. He removes the Boatman's coat and hat, puts them in the basket,
takes out the Steward's coat and hat and puts them on. He then goes to
the table, folds up the velour cloth with the inkwell and quills inside it and
puts it in the basket. A white linen cloth is on the table under the velour
cloth. He takes More's slippers from the basket then pushes the basket into
the corner down* L. *He moves the armchair down* L *of the table and turns
the chair* R *of the table to face front*)

From Richmond to Chelsea downstream, a penny ha'penny. Coat
—hat—coat—hat. From Chelsea to Richmond upstream, a penny
ha'penny. Whoever makes the regulations doesn't row a boat.
Cloth. Home again!

(*The* LIGHTS *come up. The spot fades. A clock chimes three.*   **Scene 4**
    MORE *enters* R *on the rostrum, sits wearily on the chair* R *of the table
and removes his hat. The* STEWARD *crosses to More with his slippers*)

MORE. Ah, Matthew.
STEWARD. Sir.

(*The* STEWARD *kneels and assists* MORE *to remove his shoes and put on his slippers*)

MORE. Thank you. Is Lady Alice in bed?
STEWARD. Yes, sir.
MORE. Lady Margaret?
STEWARD. No, sir. Master Roper's here.
MORE (*surprised*) At this hour? Who let him in?
STEWARD. He's a hard man to keep out, sir.
MORE. Where are they?

(MARGARET *and* WILLIAM ROPER *enter* L *and stand above the table.* ROPER *is* L *of Margaret. He is in his early thirties and has a stiff body and an immobile face. He has little imagination, a moderate brain, but an all-consuming rectitude which is his cross, his solace, and his hobby*)

MARGARET. Here, Father.
MORE (*regarding them; resignedly*) Good morning, William. Thank you, Matthew.

(*The* STEWARD *rises, picks up More's hat, crosses and exits down* L)

It's a little early for breakfast.
ROPER (*solidly*) I haven't come for breakfast, sir.

(MORE *looks at Roper and sighs*)

MARGARET (*moving to* L *of More*) Will wants to marry me, Father.
MORE. Well, he can't marry you.
ROPER. Sir Thomas, I'm to be called to the Bar.
MORE (*warmly*) Oh, congratulations, Roper.
ROPER. My family may not be at the Palace, sir, but in the City . . .
MORE. The Ropers were advocates when the Mores were selling pewter; there's nothing wrong with your family. There's nothing wrong with your fortune—there's nothing wrong with you—(*sourly*) except you need a clock . . .
ROPER. I can buy a clock, sir.
MORE. Roper, the answer's "no". (*Firmly*) And will be "no" so long as you're a heretic.
ROPER (*firing*) That's a word I don't like, Sir Thomas.
MORE. It's not a likeable word. (*He comes to life*) It's not a likeable thing.

(MARGARET *is alarmed, and from behind More's back, tries to silence Roper*)

ROPER (*moving down* L *of the table*) The Church is heretical! Doctor Luther's proved that to my satisfaction.

MORE. Luther's an excommunicate.

ROPER (*moving above the armchair*) From a heretic Church! Church? It's a shop! Forgiveness by the florin! Joblots now in Germany! Mmm, and divorces. (*He moves below the table*)

MORE (*expressionless*) Divorces?

ROPER. Oh, half England's buzzing with that.

MORE. "Half England." The Inns of Court may be buzzing. England doesn't buzz so easily.

ROPER. It will. And is that a Church? Is that a Cardinal? Is that a Pope? Or Antichrist?

(MORE *looks up angrily.* MARGARET *signals frantically*)

(*To Margaret*) Look, what I know—I'll say.

MARGARET. You've no sense of the *place*.

MORE (*ruefully*) He's no sense of the time.

ROPER. I . . .

(MORE *gently holds up his hand*)

MORE. Listen, Roper. Two years ago you were a passionate Churchman; now you're a passionate—Lutheran. We must just pray, that when your head's finished turning, your face is to the front again.

ROPER. Don't lengthen your prayers with *me*, sir.

MORE. Oh, one more or less . . . Is your horse here?

ROPER. No, I walked.

MORE. Well, take a horse from the stables and get back home.

(ROPER *crosses below More to the steps then hesitates*)

Go along.

ROPER. May I come again?

(MORE *indicates Margaret*)

MARGARET (*moving towards Roper*) Yes. Soon.

ROPER. Good night, sir.

(ROPER *exits* R *on the rostrum*)

MARGARET (*moving to* R *of More*) Is that final, Father?

MORE. As long as he's a heretic, Meg, that's absolute. (*Warmly*) Nice boy. Terribly strong principles, though. I told you to go to bed.

MARGARET. Yes. Why?

MORE (*lightly*) Because I intended you to *go* to bed. You're very pensive.

MARGARET. You're very gay. Did he talk about the divorce?

MORE (*rising and crossing to* LC) Mm? You know, I think we've been on the wrong track with Will. It's no good arguing with a Roper.

MARGARET. Father—did he?

MORE. *Old* Roper was just the same. Now, let him think he's going *with* the current and he'll turn round and start swimming in the opposite direction. What we want is a really substantial attack on the Church.

MARGARET. We're going to get it, aren't we?

MORE. Margaret, I'll not have you talk treason. And I'll not have you repeat lawyer's gossip. (*He moves to the armchair*) I'm a lawyer myself and I know what it's worth.

ALICE (*off; indignant and excited*) Thomas!

MORE. Now look what you've done.

(ALICE *enters at the top of the stairway. She is in her nightgown*)

ALICE (*descending the stairway*) Young Roper! I've just seen young Roper. On *my* horse.

MORE. He'll bring it back, dear. He's been to see Margaret.

ALICE. Oh—why you don't beat that girl . . .

MORE. No, no, she's full of education—and it's a delicate commodity. (*He sits in the armchair*)

ALICE (*moving below the table*) Mm! And more's the pity!

MORE. Yes, but it's there now and think what it cost. (*He sneezes*)

ALICE (*pouncing*) Ah! Margaret—hot water.

(MARGARET *exits* L)

MORE. I'm sorry you were awakened, chick.

ALICE (*gently*) I wasn't sleeping very deeply. Thomas—what did Wolsey want? (*She sits* R *of the table*)

MORE (*innocently*) Young Roper asked me for Margaret.

ALICE. What? Impudence!

MORE (*innocently*) Yes, wasn't it?

(MORE *has overdone it and* ALICE *glances suspiciously at him*)

ALICE (*smiling*) Old fox! (*Gently*) What did he want, Thomas?

MORE. He wanted me to read a dispatch.

ALICE. Was that all?

MORE. A Latin dispatch.

ALICE (*quietly*) You don't want to talk about it?

MORE (*gently*) No.

(MARGARET *enters* L, *carrying a pewter mug*)

ALICE. Norfolk was speaking for you as Chancellor before he left.

MORE. He's a dangerous friend, then. Wolsey's Chancellor, God help him. We don't want another.

(MARGARET *hands the mug to More*)

(*He sniffs the mug*) I don't want this.

ALICE. Drink it. Great men get colds in the head just the same as commoners.

MORE (*rising and crossing to Alice*) That's dangerous, levelling talk, Alice. Beware of the Tower.

ALICE. Drink it.

MORE. I will, I'll drink it in bed. (*He picks up his shoes*)

(ALICE *rises and exits up the stairway.* MORE *follows Alice up the stairway, carrying his shoes and mug*)

MARGARET (*following More*) Would you want to be Chancellor?

MORE. No.

MARGARET. That's what I said. But Norfolk said if Wolsey fell . . .

MORE (*no longer flippant*) If Wolsey fell, the splash would swamp a few small boats like ours. There will be no new Chancellors while Wolsey lives.

(MORE *and* MARGARET *exit at the top of the stairway. The* LIGHTS BLACK-OUT, *then a spot comes on illuminating a bright circle below the steps. Into this bright circle, from the flies, falls a great red robe and a Cardinal's hat. The vertical spot* L *comes on.*

The COMMON MAN *enters* L, *crosses, collects the robe and hat and roughly piles them into his basket. He then takes the cloth from the table and throws it into the basket. He takes a pair of spectacles and a book from the basket, puts on the spectacles and opens the book. The circle of light* RC, *fades*)

COMMON MAN (*reading*) "Whether we follow tradition in ascribing Wolsey's death to a broken heart, or accept Professor Larcomb's less feeling diagnosis of pulmonary pneumonia, its effective cause was the King's displeasure. He died at Leicester on the twenty-ninth of November, fifteen-thirty, while on his way to the Tower under charge of High Treason. England's next Lord Chancellor was Sir Thomas More, a scholar and, by popular repute, a saint. His scholarship is supported by his writings; saintliness is a quality less easy to establish. But from his wilful indifference to realities which were obvious to quite ordinary contemporaries, it seems all too probable that he had it."

(*The* COMMON MAN *removes his spectacles, throws them with the book into the basket and exits down* L, *taking the basket with him. A screen, depicting Hampton Court, is lowered from the flies and rests on the rostrum up* RC. *The spot down* L *fades and the* LIGHTS *come up for the Hampton Court scene.* **Scene 5**

CROMWELL *enters* R *on the rostrum.*

RICH *enters up* R *and crosses to* L)

CROMWELL. Rich!

(RICH *stops, turns, sees Cromwell and smiles willingly*)

What brings you to Hampton? (*He sits on the steps*)
RICH (*crossing below the table to* C) I came with the Duke last night,
Master Cromwell. They're hunting again.
CROMWELL. It's a kingly pastime, Master Rich.

(*They both smile*)

I'm glad you found employment. You're the Duke's secretary, are
you not?
RICH (*flustered*) My work *is* mostly secretarial.
CROMWELL (*as one making an effort of memory*) Or is it his librarian
you are?
RICH. I do look after His Grace's library, yes.
CROMWELL. Oh. Well, that's something. And I don't suppose
you're bothered much by His Grace—in the library?

(RICH *smiles uncertainly*)

It's odd how differently men's futures flow. My late master died in
disgrace, and here I am in the King's own service. There you are,
in a *comparative* backwater—yet the new Lord Chancellor's an old
friend of yours. (*He looks directly at Rich*)
RICH (*uncertainly*) He isn't really my *friend*.
CROMWELL. Oh, I thought he was. (*He prepares to go*)
RICH. In a sense he is.
CROMWELL (*reproachfully*) Well, I always understood he set you
up in life.
RICH. Master Cromwell—what *is* it that you do for the King?

(CHAPUYS *and his* ATTENDANT *enter down* R *and stand* R *of the
steps*)

CHAPUYS (*roguishly*) Yes, *I* should like to know that, Master
Cromwell.
CROMWELL (*rising*) Ah, Signor Chapuys. You've met His Excel-
lency, Rich? (*He indicates Chapuys*) Signor Chapuys, the Spanish
Ambassador. (*He indicates Rich*) The Duke of Norfolk's librarian.
CHAPUYS. But how should we introduce *you*, Master Cromwell, if
we had the happiness?
CROMWELL. Oh, sly! (*He crosses to* L *of Rich*) Do you notice how
sly he is, Rich? Well, I suppose you would call me—(*he turns suddenly*)
"The King's Ear". (*He shrugs deprecatingly*) It's a useful organ—the
ear. But in fact it's even simpler than that. (*He crosses to* R *of Rich*)
When the King wants something done, I do it.
CHAPUYS. Ah! (*He moves to* R *of Cromwell. With mock interest*) But
then why these Justices, Chancellors, Admirals?
CROMWELL. Oh, they are the Constitution. Our ancient, English
Constitution. I merely do things.
CHAPUYS. For example, Master Cromwell . . . ?
CROMWELL (*admiringly*) Oho—beware these professional diplo-

mats. Well now, for example; next week at Deptford we are launching the *Great Harry*—one thousand tons, four masts, sixty-six guns, an overall length of one hundred and seventy-five feet. It's expected to be very effective—all this you probably know. (*He crosses below Chapuys to* R *of the steps*) However, you may not know that the King himself will guide her down the river; yes, the King himself will be her pilot. He will have assistance, of course, but he himself will be her pilot. He will have a pilot's whistle upon which he will blow, and he will wear in every respect a common pilot's uniform. (*He crosses below Chapuys to* R *of Rich*) Except for the material, which will be cloth of gold. These innocent fancies require more preparation than you might suppose and someone has to do it. (*He spreads his hands and crosses down* L) Meanwhile, I do prepare myself for—higher things. I stock my mind.

CHAPUYS. Alas, Master Cromwell, don't we all. (*He crosses to* R *of Cromwell*) This ship, for instance—it has fifty-six guns by the way, not sixty-six and only forty of them are heavy—after the launching I understand——

(CROMWELL'S *face darkens*)

—the King will take his barge to Chelsea.
CROMWELL (*sharply*) Yes.
CHAPUYS. To . . .
CROMWELL. Sir Thomas More's.
CHAPUYS (*sweetly*) Will you be there?
CROMWELL. Oh, no—they'll talk about the divorce.

(CHAPUYS, *shocked, turns away* R. RICH *draws uneasily away up* C)

The King will ask him for an answer.
CHAPUYS (*ruffled*) He has given his answer.
CROMWELL. The King will ask him for another.
CHAPUYS. Sir Thomas is a good son of the Church.
CROMWELL. Sir Thomas is a man.

(*The* STEWARD *enters down the stairway, crosses the rostrum in front of the screen to* R *of it, crosses behind the screen to* C, *passes under the stairway and stands* L *of the table*. CHAPUYS *and* CROMWELL *look sharply at the Steward, then at one another*)

CHAPUYS (*innocently*) Isn't that his steward, now?
CROMWELL. I believe it is. Well, good day, Your Excellency.
CHAPUYS (*eagerly*) Good day, Master Cromwell. (*He expects Cromwell to go*)
CROMWELL (*standing firm*) Good day.

(CHAPUYS *has to go. He and the* ATTENDANT *go behind the screen, whence they remain in sight of the audience. The* STEWARD *crosses to* R *of Cromwell*)

STEWARD (*conspiratorially*) Sir, Sir Thomas doesn't talk about it.
(*He waits*)

(CROMWELL *remains stony*)

He doesn't talk about it, to his wife, sir. (*He waits*)
CROMWELL. This is worth nothing.
STEWARD (*crossing to* L *of Cromwell; significantly*) But he doesn't
talk about it to Lady Margaret—that's his daughter, sir.
CROMWELL. So?
STEWARD. So he's worried, sir.

(CROMWELL *is interested*)

Frightened.

(CROMWELL *takes out a coin but pauses suspiciously*)

Sir, he goes *white* when it's mentioned.
CROMWELL (*handing the coin to the Steward*) All right. (*He moves
down* R)
STEWARD (*looking at the coin; reproachfully*) Oh, sir . . .
CROMWELL (*waving the Steward away*) Are you coming in my
direction, Rich?
RICH (*still hanging off*) No, no.

(*The* STEWARD *moves to* R *of the steps*)

CROMWELL. I think you should, you know.

(CROMWELL *exits* R)

RICH. I can't tell you anything. (*He stands up* C, *under the stairway,
and listens to the following dialogue*)

(CHAPUYS *and the* ATTENDANT *come from behind the screen.* CHAPUYS
stands on the bottom step of the steps RC *and the* ATTENDANT *on the third*)

CHAPUYS (*to the Steward*) Well?
STEWARD. Sir Thomas rises at six, sir, and prays for an hour and
a half.
CHAPUYS. Yes?
STEWARD. During Lent, sir, he lived entirely on bread and water.
CHAPUYS. Yes?
STEWARD. He goes to confession twice a week, sir. Parish priest.
Dominican.
CHAPUYS. Ah. He is a true son of the Church.
STEWARD (*soapy*) That he is, sir.
CHAPUYS. What did Master Cromwell want?
STEWARD. Same as you, sir.
CHAPUYS. No man can serve two masters, Steward.
STEWARD. No, indeed, sir; I serve *one*. (*He pulls to the front an*

enormous cross until then hanging at his back on a length of string, a wooden caricature of the ebony cross worn by Chapuys)

CHAPUYS. Good, simple man. Here. (*He gives the Steward a coin*) Peace be with you.
STEWARD. And ·with you, sir.
CHAPUYS. Our Lord watch you.
STEWARD. You, too, sir.

(CHAPUYS *exits* R *on the rostrum.*
The ATTENDANT *follows him off*)

That's a very religious man. (*He crosses to* C)
RICH (*stepping forward*) Matthew.

(*The* STEWARD *stops* C, *below the table*)

(*He moves to* R *of the Steward*) What does Signor Chapuys want?
STEWARD. I've no idea, sir.
RICH (*handing the Steward a coin*) What did you tell him?
STEWARD. I told him that Sir Thomas says his prayers and goes to confession.
RICH. Why that?
STEWARD. That's what he wanted to know, sir. I mean, I could have told him any number of things about Sir Thomas—that he has rheumatism, prefers red wine to white, is easily seasick, fond of kippers, afraid of drowning. But that's what he wanted to know, sir.
RICH. What did he say?
STEWARD. He said that Sir Thomas is a good churchman, sir?
RICH (*crossing below the Steward to* L) Well, that's true, isn't it?
STEWARD (*moving to* R *of Rich*) I'm just telling you what he said, sir. (*He points* R) Master Cromwell went that way, sir.
RICH (*furiously*) Did I ask you which way Master Cromwell went?

(RICH *exits down* L. *The* STEWARD *moves* C)

STEWARD (*to the audience; thoughtfully*) The great thing's not to get out of your depth. What I can tell them's common knowledge. But now they've given money for it and everyone wants value for his money. They'll make a secret of it now to prove they've not been bilked. They'll make it a secret by making it dangerous. Mm. Oh, when I can't touch the bottom I'll go deaf, blind and dumb. (*He holds out the coins*) And that's more than I *earn* in a fortnight.

(*The* STEWARD *exits down* R. *The Hampton Court screen is taken out and a border of flowers is lowered from the flies. The* LIGHTS *change for the Garden Scene. The back of the stage becomes a source of glittering green-yellow. A fanfare of trumpets is heard in the distance.* **Scene 6** ALICE, NORFOLK *and* MARGARET *erupt on to the stage.* ALICE *enters* R *on the rostrum.* NORFOLK *enters* L. MARGARET *enters at the top of the stairway*)

ALICE (*on the rostrum; distressed*) No sign of him, my Lord.
NORFOLK (*crossing to* C) God's body, Alice, he must be found.
ALICE (*to Margaret*) He *must* be in the house.
MARGARET (*descending the stairway*) He's *not* in the house, Mother.
ALICE. Then he must be here in the garden. (*She comes down the steps and stands up* C)

(MARGARET *moves to Alice*)

NORFOLK (*crossing to* L *of the steps*) He takes things too far, Alice.
ALICE. Do I not know it?
NORFOLK. It will end badly for him.
ALICE. I know that, too.

(*The* STEWARD *enters down* R *and moves to* R *of the steps.* ALICE *and* MARGARET *turn and stand behind the table*)

MARGARET ⎫ ⎧Mathew! Where's my father?
NORFOLK ⎬ (*together*) ⎨Where's your master?
ALICE ⎭ ⎩Where is Sir Thomas?

(*A fanfare of trumpets is heard, shorter but nearer*)

NORFOLK (*despairingly*) Oh, my God!
ALICE. Oh, Jesus!
STEWARD. My lady—the King?
NORFOLK. Yes, fool. (*Threateningly*) And if the King arrives and the Chancellor's not here . . .
STEWARD. Sir, my lady, it's not *my* fault.

(*The* STEWARD *goes on to the rostrum and exits* R)

NORFOLK (*quietly displeased*) Lady Alice, Thomas'll get no good of it. This is not how Wolsey made himself great.
ALICE (*stiffly*) Thomas has his own way of doing things, my Lord.
NORFOLK (*testily*) Yes, yes, Thomas is unique; but where *is* Thomas?

(*The* STEWARD *wheels a small chapel door on to the right end of the rostrum. Plainsong is heard.* NORFOLK *and* ALICE, *on a common impulse, go quickly on to the rostrum.* NORFOLK *opens the door. The plainsong is louder*)

ALICE (L *of Norfolk; looking off* R) Thomas!
MARGARET (*moving to* L *of the rostrum*) Father!
NORFOLK (*standing above the doorway; indignantly*) My Lord Chancellor!

(MORE *enters through the chapel door. He blinks in the light. He is wearing a cassock. The door closes behind him. The plainsong ceases*)

What sort of fooling is this? Does the King visit you every day?

MORE (*crossing below Norfolk to* L *of him*) No, but I go to Vespers most days.

NORFOLK. He's here!

MORE. But isn't this visit *meant* to be a surprise?

NORFOLK (*grimly*) For you, yes, not for him.

MARGARET (*crossing to* R *of the steps*) Father . . . (*She indicates More's cassock*)

NORFOLK (*coming down the steps*) Yes—d'you propose to meet the King disguised as a parish clerk? (*He crosses to* LC)

(MARGARET *goes on to the rostrum. She and* ALICE *fall upon More and drag the cassock over his head*)

A parish clerk, my Lord Chancellor! You dishonour the King and his office.

MORE (*appearing momentarily in the folds of the cassock*) The service of God is not a dishonour to any office.

(*The cassock is pulled off and* MARGARET *hands it to the Steward*)

Believe me, my friend, I do not belittle the honour His Majesty is doing me. (*Briskly*) Well! That's a lovely dress, Alice; so's that, Margaret. (*He comes down the steps*)

(ALICE *follows More down the steps.*
The STEWARD *wheels the chapel door off* R, *taking the cassock with him*)

(*He looks at* Norfolk) I'm a dowdy bird, aren't I? (*He looks at* Alice) Calm yourself, Alice, we're all ready now. (*He turns about and it is seen that his gown is caught up behind him revealing his spindly legs in long hose laced up at the thighs*)

ALICE. Thomas!

(MARGARET *laughs and follows* MORE *and* ALICE *down* C)

MORE. What's the matter?

(MORE *turns round again.* ALICE *and* MARGARET *pursue him to pull down the gown while* NORFOLK *throws his hands in the air. There is expostulation, explanation and exclamation, overlapping in a babble*)

NORFOLK. By God, you can be hare-brained!

MARGARET. Be still.

ALICE. Oh, Thomas, Thomas!

NORFOLK. What whim possessed you . . . ?

MORE. 'Twas not a whim.

ALICE. Your second-best stockings!

MARGARET. Father, be still!

NORFOLK. Oh, enough's enough!

MORE. Haven't you done?

(*A fanfare of trumpets is heard.* NORFOLK *kneels down* L. MARGARET *kneels* R *of Norfolk.* MORE *kneels* C. ALICE *kneels* R *of the steps. They all face the rostrum.*

KING HENRY THE EIGHTH *enters at the top of the stairway and comes half-way down. He is not the Holbein Henry, but a much younger man, clean-shaven, bright-eyed, graceful and athletic. The Golden Hope of the New Learning throughout Europe. Only the levity with which he handles his absolute power foreshadows his future corruption. His clothing is of cloth of gold, and he has a whistle on a gold cord around his neck. In the silence he descends slowly to the rostrum, blowing softly on his whistle*)

Your Majesty does my house more honour than I fear my household can bear.

(HENRY *comes down the steps to* R *of More and raises him*)

HENRY. No ceremony, Thomas. No ceremony.

(ALICE, MARGARET *and* NORFOLK *rise*)

A passing fancy—I happened to be on the river. (*He displays one of his shoes. Proudly*) Look—mud.

MORE. We do it in better style, Your Grace, when we come by the road.

HENRY. Oh, the road! There's the road for me, Thomas, the river; *my* river. By Heaven, what an evening! (*He crosses to* L *of Alice*) I fear we come upon you unexpectedly, Lady Alice.

ALICE (*shocked*) Oh, no, Your Grace—(*she remembers*) that is—yes, but we are ready for you—ready to entertain Your Grace, that is.

MORE. This is my daughter Margaret, sir.

(MARGARET *curtsies low*)

She has not had the honour to meet Your Grace.

(HENRY *crosses below More to* R *of Margaret and looks her over*)

HENRY. Why, Margaret, they told me you were a scholar.

(MARGARET *is confused*)

MORE. Answer, Margaret.

MARGARET. Among women I pass for one, Your Grace.

(NORFOLK *and* ALICE *exchange approving glances.* HENRY *speaks Latin, a brief sentence.* MARGARET *replies even more briefly.* HENRY *speaks a longer sentence.* MARGARET *replies at length. Her Latin is better than his, and he is not altogether pleased*)

HENRY. *Antiquone modo Latine loqueris, an Oxoniensi?* (*Is your Latin the old Latin, or the Oxford Latin?*)

MARGARET. *Quem me docuit pater, domine.* (*My father's Latin, Sire*)

HENRY. *Bene. Optimus est. Graecamne linguam quoque te docuit?* (*Good. That is the best. And has he taught you Greek, too?*)

MARGARET. *Graecam me docuit non pater meus sed mei patris amicus. Johannes Coletus, Sancti Pauli Decanus. In litteris Graecis tamen, non minus quam Latinus. Ars magistri minuitur discipuli stultitia.* (*Not my father, Sire, but my father's friend. John Colet, Deacon of St Paul's. But it is with the Greek as it is with the Latin; the skill of the master is lost in the pupil's lack of it*)

HENRY. Ho! (*He crosses down* L, *talking to More*) Take care, Thomas——

(MARGARET *begins to rise from her curtsy.* MORE *gently presses her down again before Henry turns*)

—too much reading is a weariness of the flesh, and there is no end to the making of books. (*He turns to Margaret*) Can you dance, too?

MARGARET. Not well, Your Grace.

HENRY. Well, *I* dance superlatively. (*He crosses to* L *of Margaret and plants his leg before her face*) That's a dancer's *leg*, Margaret.

(MARGARET *has the wit to look straight up and smile at Henry.* NORFOLK *grins the grin of a comrade*)

(*All good humour, he pulls Margaret to her feet and sees Norfolk's grin*) Hey, Norfolk? (*He indicates Norfolk's leg with much distaste*) Now, *that's* a wrestler's leg. But I can throw him. (*He seizes Norfolk*) Shall I show them, Howard?

(NORFOLK *is alarmed for his dignity*)

(*To Margaret*) Shall I?

MARGARET (*looking at Norfolk; gently*) No, Your Grace.

(HENRY *releases* NORFOLK *who moves behind the table*)

HENRY (*seriously*) You are gentle. (*To More. Approvingly*) That's good. (*To Margaret*) You shall read to me.

(MARGARET *is about to demur*)

No, no, you shall read to me. (*He crosses below More to* L *of Alice*) Lady Alice, the river's given me an appetite.

ALICE. If Your Grace would share a very simple supper . . .

HENRY. It would please me to. (*He prepares to lead off but stops, turns and crosses below More to* R *of Margaret*) I'm something of a scholar, too; did you know?

MARGARET. All the world knows Your Grace's book, asserting the seven sacraments of the Church.

HENRY. Ah, yes. Between ourselves, your father had a hand in that—eh, Thomas?

MORE. Here and there, Your Grace. In a minor capacity.

HENRY (*looking at More*) He seeks to shame me with his modesty. (*He turns to Alice*) On second thoughts we'll follow Lady Alice, Thomas and I will follow. (*He waves them off and crosses to* L)

(ALICE, NORFOLK *and* MARGARET *bow and go to the rostrum.* ALICE *starts up the stairway and* NORFOLK *follows her*)

(*Suddenly*) Wait! (*He raises his whistle to his lips*)

(ALICE *stops on the second step of the stairway,* NORFOLK *stops at the foot of the stairway and* MARGARET *stops at the top of the steps*)

(*He crosses to* L *of Margaret*) Margaret, are you fond of music?
MARGARET. Yes, Your Grace.
HENRY (*holding out the whistle*) Blow.

(MARGARET *is uncertain*)

Blow.

(MARGARET *blows the whistle*)

Louder.

(MARGARET *blows louder and at once, music is heard off, stately and oversweet. There are expressions of pleasure all round*)

I brought them with me, Lady Alice; take them in.

(ALICE, NORFOLK *and* MARGARET *exit up the stairway. The music very slowly recedes*)

(*He crosses to* L) Listen to this, Thomas. (*He beats time*) Do you know it?
MORE. No, Your Grace, I . . .
HENRY. Listen!

(MORE *is silent*)

(*He goes on with his listening*) I launched a ship, today, Thomas.
MORE. Yes, Your Grace, I . . .
HENRY. *Listen.* (*He pauses*) The *Great Harry.* I steered her, Thomas, under sail.
MORE. You have many accomplishments, Your Grace.
HENRY (*holding up a finger for silence*) Listen, man, listen. (*He pauses*) A great experience.

(MORE *is silent*)

A great experience, Thomas.
MORE. Yes, Your Grace.

(*The music grows fainter*)

HENRY (*moving to* L *of More*) I am a fool.
MORE. How so, Your Grace?

(*There is a pause, during which the music fades to silence*)

HENRY. What else but a fool to live in a Court, in a licentious mob—when I have friends, with gardens.

MORE. Your Grace . . .

HENRY. No courtship, no ceremony, Thomas. Be seated.

(MORE *sits in the armchair*)

(*He stands below the right end of the table*) You *are* my friend, are you not?

MORE. Your Majesty.

HENRY. And thank God I have a friend for my Chancellor. (*He laughs*) Readier to be friends, I trust, than he was to be Chancellor. (*He moves to* R *of More*)

MORE. My own knowledge of my poor abilities . . .

HENRY (*moving* R *of the table*) I will judge of your abilities, Thomas. (*He crosses above the table to* L *of it*) Did you know that Wolsey named you for Chancellor?

MORE. Wolsey!

HENRY. Aye; before he died. Wolsey named you and Wolsey was no fool.

MORE. He was a statesman of incomparable ability, Your Grace.

HENRY. Was he? (*He crosses below More to the table and sits on the downstage edge of it*) Was he so?

(MORE *rises*)

Then why did he fail me? Be seated——

(MORE *resumes his seat*)

—it was villainy, then. Yes—villainy. I was right to break him; he was all pride, Thomas; a proud man; pride right through. And he failed me.

(MORE *opens his mouth to speak*)

He failed me in the one thing that mattered. The one thing that matters, Thomas, then or now. And why? (*He rises and crosses to* RC) He wanted to be Pope. Yes, he wanted to be the Bishop of Rome. (*He crosses to* R *of More*) I'll tell you something, Thomas, and you can check this for yourself—it was never merry in England while we had cardinals amongst us. (*He nods significantly at More*)

(MORE *lowers his eyes*)

But look now—(*he moves* C *and turns to More*) I shall forget the feel of that—great tiller under my hands—I took her down to Dogget's Bank, went about and brought her up in Tilbury Roads. A man could sail clean round the world in that ship.

MORE (*with affectionate admiration*) Some men could, Your Grace.

HENRY (*crossing down* L; *offhandedly*) Touching that matter of my divorce, Thomas; have you thought of it since we last talked?

MORE. Of little else.

HENRY (*moving to* L *of the table*) Then you see your way clear to me?

MORE. That you should put away Queen Catherine, Sire? Oh, alas—(*he thumps the arms of his chair in distress*) as I think of it I see so clearly that I can *not* come with Your Grace, that my endeavour is not to think of it at all.

HENRY (*moving above the table*) Then you have not thought enough. (*With real appeal*) Great God, Thomas, why do you hold out against me in the desire of my heart—the very wick of my heart? (*He takes out his dagger and plays with it*)

MORE (*drawing up his sleeve and baring his arm*) There is my right arm. (*A practical proposition*) Take your dagger and saw it from my shoulder, and I will laugh and be thankful, if by that means I can come with Your Grace with a clear conscience.

HENRY (*pulling uncomfortably at the sleeve*) I know it, Thomas, I know.

MORE (*rising; formally*) I crave pardon if I offend.

HENRY (*suspiciously*) Speak, then.

MORE. When I took the Great Seal, Your Majesty promised not to pursue me on this matter.

HENRY (*driving his dagger into the table*) Ha! So I break my word, Master More! (*He withdraws the dagger*) No, no, I'm joking—I joke roughly. (*He wanders away* L) I often think I'm a rough fellow. Yes, a rough young fellow. (*He shakes his head indulgently*) Be seated.

(MORE *sits* R *of the table*)

(*He looks at the flower border*) That's a Rose Bey. We have one like it at Hampton—not so red as that, though. Ha—I'm in an excellent frame of mind. (*He glances again at the flowers*) Beautiful! (*Reasonable and pleasant*) You must consider, Thomas, that I stand in peril of my soul. It was no marriage; she was my brother's widow. *Leviticus:* "Thou shalt not uncover the nakedness of thy brother's wife." *Leviticus*, chapter eighteen, verse sixteen.

MORE. Yes, Your Grace. But *Deuteronomy* . . .

HENRY (*crossing to* RC; *triumphantly*) *Deuteronomy's* ambiguous.

MORE (*bursting out*) Your Grace, I'm not fitted to meddle in these matters—to me it seems a question for the Holy See.

HENRY (*reprovingly*) Thomas, Thomas, does a man need a Pope to tell him when he's sinned? It was a sin, Thomas; I admit it; I repent. (*He crosses and sits in the armchair*) And God has punished me. Son after son she's borne me, Thomas, all dead at birth, or dead within the month; I never saw the hand of God so clear in anything. I have a daughter, she's a good child, a well-set child—but I have no son. (*He flares up*) It is my bounden *duty* to put away the Queen and all the Popes back to St Peter shall not come between me and my duty. How is it that you cannot see? Everyone else does.

MORE (*eagerly*) Then why does Your Grace need my poor support?

HENRY. Because you are honest. What's more to the purpose, you're known to be honest. There are those like Norfolk who follow me because I wear the crown, and there are those like Master Cromwell who follow me because they are jackals with sharp teeth and I am their lion, and there is a mass that follows me because it follows anything that moves—and there is you.

MORE. I am sick to think how much I must displease Your Grace.

HENRY. No, Thomas, I respect your sincerity. Respect? Oh, man, it's water in the desert. (*He pauses briefly*) How did you like our music? That air they played, it had a certain—well, tell me what you thought of it.

MORE (*relieved at this turn; smiling*) Could it have been Your Grace's own?

HENRY (*smiling*) Discovered! Now I'll never know your true opinion. And that's irksome, Thomas, for we artists, though we love praise, yet we love truth better.

MORE (*mildly*) Then I will tell Your Grace truly what I thought of it.

HENRY (*a little disconcerted*) Speak, then.

MORE. To me it seemed—delightful.

HENRY. Thomas—I chose the right man for Chancellor.

MORE. I must in fairness add that my taste in music is reputedly deplorable.

HENRY (*laughing*) Your taste in music is excellent. It exactly coincides with my own. (*He rises*) Ah, music! Music! Send them back without me, Thomas; I will live here in Chelsea and make music.

MORE. My house is at Your Grace's disposal.

HENRY (*sitting on the downstage edge of the table*) Thomas, you me, we will stay here together and make music.

MORE. Will Your Grace honour my roof after dinner?

HENRY (*rising and moving down L*) Mm? Yes: I expect I'll bellow for you.

MORE. My wife will be more . . .

HENRY. Yes, yes. (*He turns, his face set*) Touching this other business, mark you, Thomas, I'll have no opposition.

MORE (*sadly*) Your Grace?

HENRY (*pacing up L*) No opposition, I say! No opposition. Your conscience is your own affair; but you are my Chancellor. There, you have my word—I'll leave you out of it. (*He stands behind the table*) But I don't take it kindly, Thomas, and I'll have no opposition. (*He paces down R*) I see how it will be; the Bishops will oppose me. The full-fed, hypocritical "Princes of the Church". Ha! (*He paces across to L*) As for the Pope! Am I to burn in Hell because the Bishop of Rome with the Emperor's knife to his throat, mouths me *Deuteronomy?* (*He paces up L*) Hypocrites!

(MORE *rises*)

They're all hypocrites! Mind they do not take you in, Thomas. (*He paces down* c) Lie low, if you will, but I'll brook no opposition— no words, no signs, no letters, no pamphlets—mark it, Thomas—no writings against me.

MORE. Your Grace is unjust. I am Your Grace's loyal minister. If I cannot serve Your Grace in this great matter of the Queen . . .

HENRY. I have no Queen. Catherine is not my wife and no priest can make her so, and they that say she is my wife lie and are traitors. Mind it, Thomas.

MORE (*his voice unsteady*) Am I a babbler, Your Grace?

HENRY. You are stubborn. (*He sits in the armchair. Wooingly*) If you could come with me, you are the man I would soonest raise—yes, with my own hand.

MORE (*sitting* R *of the table and covering his face*) Oh, Your Grace overwhelms me.

(*A complicated chiming of little bells is heard chiming eight*)

HENRY. What's that?

MORE. Eight o'clock, Your Grace.

HENRY (*uneasily eyeing More*) Oh, lift yourself up, man—have I not promised?

(MORE *braces himself*)

(*He rises*) Shall we eat?

MORE (*rising*) If Your Grace pleases. (*Recovering*) What will Your Grace sing for us?

HENRY. Eight o'clock, you said? Thomas, the tide will be chang- ing. I was forgetting the tide. (*He crosses to the steps*) I'd better go.

MORE (*gravely*) I'm sorry, Your Grace.

HENRY. I must catch the tide or I'll not get back to Richmond till . . .

(MORE *moves to the steps*)

No, don't come. Tell Norfolk. (*He has his foot on the bottom step*)

(ALICE *enters at the top of the stairway*)

(*He goes up the stairway*) Oh, Lady Alice, I must go. (*He passes Alice on the stairway and turns*) I must catch the tide. To tell the truth, Lady Alice, I have forgotten in your haven here, how time flows past out- side. Affairs call me to court and so I give you my thanks and say good night. (*He continues up the stairway*)

(ALICE *and* MORE *bow*)

ALICE }
MORE } (*together*) Good night, Your Grace.

(HENRY *exits at the top of the stairway*)

ALICE (*descending the stairway*) What's this? You crossed him.
MORE. Somewhat.
ALICE. Why?
MORE (*apologetically*) I couldn't find the other way.
ALICE (*angrily*) You're too nice altogether, Thomas. (*She reaches the bottom of the steps*)
MORE. Woman, mind your house.
ALICE (*moving to* R *of More*) I *am* minding my house.
MORE (*taking in her anxiety*) Well, Alice—what would you *want* me to do?
ALICE. Be ruled! If you won't rule him, be ruled.
MORE (*quietly*) I neither could nor would rule my King.

(ALICE *turns away* R)

(*Pleasantly*) But there's a little—little area where I must rule myself. It's very little—less to him than a tennis court.

(ALICE's *face is still full of foreboding*)

(*He sighs*) Look; it was eight o'clock. (*He takes Alice's shoulders*) At eight o'clock, Lady Anne likes to dance.
ALICE (*relieved*) Oh?
MORE. I think so.
ALICE (*irritably*) And *you* stand between them. (*She moves down* R)
MORE. I? What stands between them is a sacrament of the Church. I'm less important than you think, Alice.
ALICE (*appealing*) Thomas, stay friends with him.
MORE. Whatever can be done by smiling, you may relay on me to do.
ALICE. You don't know *how* to flatter.
MORE. I flatter very well. My recipe's beginning to be widely copied. It's the basic syrup with just a soupçon of discreet impudence . . .
ALICE (*still uneasy*) I wish he'd eaten here.
MORE. Yes—we shall be living on that "simple supper" of yours for a fortnight.

(ALICE *will not laugh*)

Alice.

(ALICE *will not turn to him*)

Alice.

(ALICE *turns*)

Set your mind at rest—this—(*he taps himself*) is not the stuff of which martyrs are made. (*He moves down* L)
ROPER (*off*) Sir Thomas!
MORE (*wincing*) Oh, no! (*He moves* C)

(ROPER *and* MARGARET *enter at the top of the stairway and descend*)

ALICE (*sitting on the bench* R) Will Roper, whatd'you want?

MARGARET. William, I told you not to.

ROPER. I'm not easily "told", Meg.

MARGARET. I *asked* you not to.

ROPER (*indicating his throat*) Meg, I'm full to here.

MARGARET. It's not convenient.

ROPER. Must everything be made convenient? I'm not a convenient man, Meg—I've got an inconvenient conscience. (*He moves down* C)

(MARGARET *gestures helplessly to More and stands on the rostrum*)

MORE (*laughing*) Joshua's trumpet. One note on that brass conscience of yours and my daughter's walls are down.

ROPER. You raised her, sir.

MORE (*a little puzzled*) How long have you been here? Are you in the King's party?

ROPER. No, sir, I am *not* in the King's party. It's of that I wish to speak to you. My spirit is perturbed.

MORE (*suppressing a grin*) Is it, Will? Why?

ROPER (*moving to* R *of More*) I've been offered a seat in the next Parliament.

(MORE *looks up sharply*)

Ought I to take it?

MORE. No. Well, that depends. With your views on Church Reform I should have thought you could do yourself a lot of good in the next Parliament.

ROPER (*crossing down* L) My views on the Church—I must confess —since last we met my views have somewhat modified.

(MORE *and* MARGARET *exchange a smile*)

I modify nothing concerning the *body* of the Church—the money changers in the temple must be scourged from thence—with a scourge of fire if that is necessary. But an attack on the Church herself. No, I see behind that an attack on God.

MORE. Roper!

ROPER (*moving to* L *of More*) The Devil's work.

MORE. Roper!

ROPER. To be done by the Devil's ministers.

MORE. For Heaven's sake remember my office.

ROPER. Oh, if you stand on your office . . .

MORE (*crossing below Roper to* L *of him*) I don't stand on it, but there are certain things I may not hear.

ROPER. Sophistication. It is what I was told. The Court has corrupted you, Sir Thomas; you are not the man you were; you have learnt to study your "convenience"; you have learnt to flatter.

More. There, Alice, you see? I have a reputation for it.
Alice. God's Body, young man, if I was the Chancellor, I'd have you whipped.

(*The* Steward *enters* r *on the rostrum*)

Steward. Master Rich is here, Sir Thomas.

(Rich *enters* r *on the rostrum and crosses to the top of the steps*)

Rich. Good evening, sir.
More. Ah, Richard?
Rich. Good evening, Lady Alice.

(Alice *nods non-committally*)

Lady Margaret.
Margaret (*quite friendly but very clear*) Good evening, Master Rich.

(*There is a pause*)

More. Do you know—(*he indicates* Roper) William Roper, the younger?
Rich (*moving down* rc) By reputation, of course.
Roper (*crossing to* l *of* Rich) Good evening, Master . . .
Rich. Rich.
Roper. Oh. (*He recollects something*) Oh.
Rich (*quick and hostile*) You have heard of me?
Roper (*crossing to* l *of the steps; shortly*) Yes.
Rich (*excitedly*) In what connection? I don't know what you can have heard. (*He looks around. Hotly*) I sense that I'm not welcome here.

(Rich *has jumped the gun and the others are startled*)

More (*gently*) Why, Richard, have you done something that should make you not welcome?
Rich. Why, do you suspect me of it?
More. I shall begin to.
Rich (*moving to* r *of* More; *hurriedly*) Cromwell is asking questions. About you. About you particularly.

(More *is unmoved*)

He is continually collecting information about you.

(*The* Steward *starts to ascend the stairway*)

More. I know it. (*To the* Steward) Stay a minute, Matthew.

(*The* Steward *stops on the fifth stair*)

Rich (*pointing to the* Steward) That's one of his sources.

MORE. Of course; that's one of my servants.

(*The* STEWARD *exits up the stairway*)

RICH (*in a low, hurried voice*) Signor Chapuys, the Spanish Ambassador . . .

MORE. Collects information, too. That's one of his functions. (*He looks very gravely at Rich*)

RICH (*his voice cracking*) You look at me as though I were an enemy.

MORE (*putting out a hand to steady Rich*) Why, Richard, you're shaking.

RICH. I'm adrift. Help me.

MORE. How?

RICH. Employ me.

MORE. No.

RICH (*desperately*) Employ me!

MORE. No.

(RICH *goes on to the rostrum and turns*)

RICH. I would be steadfast.

MORE. Richard, you couldn't answer for yourself even so far as tonight.

(RICH *exits* R *on the rostrum. The others watch him go, then* ALICE *and* ROPER *turn to* More, *their faces alert*)

ROPER (*with a step towards More*) Arrest him.

ALICE (*rising*) Yes.

MORE. For what?

ALICE. He's dangerous.

ROPER. For libel; he's a spy.

ALICE. He is. Arrest him.

MARGARET (*moving to* L *of the table*) Father, that man's bad.

MORE. There is no law against that.

ROPER. There is! God's law.

MORE. Then God can arrest him.

ROPER (*moving to* R *of More*) Sophistication upon sophistication.

MORE (*moving* LC) No, sheer simplicity. The law, Roper, the law. I know what's legal not what's right. I'll stick to what's legal.

ROPER. Then you set Man's law above God's!

MORE. No, far below; but let me draw your attention to a fact ---I'm *not* God. (*He moves to* L *of Roper*) The currents and eddies of right and wrong, which you find such plain-sailing, I can't navigate, I'm no voyager. But in the thickets of the law, oh, there I'm a forester. (*To himself*) I doubt if there's a man alive who could follow me there, thank God.

ALICE (*pointing after Rich; exasperated*) While you talk, he's gone. (*She moves to the steps*)

MORE (*crossing to* L *of Alice*) And go he should if he was the devil himself until he broke the law.

ROPER. So now you'd give the Devil benefit of law.

MORE (*turning to Roper*) Yes. What would you do? Cut a great road through the law to get after the Devil?

ROPER. I'd cut down every law in England to do that.

MORE (*roused and excited*) Oh? And when the last law was down— (*he moves to* R *of Roper*) and the Devil turned round on you—where would you hide, Roper, the laws all being flat? (*He crosses to* LC) This country's planted thick with laws from coast to coast—Man's laws, not God's—and if you cut them down—and you're just the man to do it—d'you really think you could stand upright in the winds that would blow then? (*Quietly*) Yes, I'd give the Devil benefit of law, for my own safety's sake.

ROPER (*moving to* R *of More*) I have long suspected this; this is the golden calf; the law's your god.

MORE (*wearily*) Oh, Roper, you're a fool, God's my god. (*Rather bitter*) But I find him rather too—(*very bitterly*) subtle—I don't know where he is nor what he wants.

ROPER. My god wants service, to the end and unremitting; nothing else.

MORE (*dryly*) Are you sure that's God? He sounds like Moloch. But indeed it may be God—and whoever hunts for me, Roper, God or Devil, will find me hiding in the thickets of the law. And I'll hide my daughter with me. Not hoist her up the mainmast of your sea-going principles. They put about too nimbly.

(MORE *exits down* L. *They all look after him*)

MARGARET (*moving to Roper and touching his hand*) Oh, that was harsh.

ROPER (*turning to Margaret; seriously*) What's happened here?

ALICE (*turning away; her voice strained*) He can't abide a fool, that's all. Be off.

ROPER (*to Margaret*) "Hide you." Hide you from what?

ALICE (*turning; near to tears*) He said nothing about hiding me, you noticed. I've got too fat to hide, I suppose.

MARGARET (*moving to the steps*) You know he meant us both.

ROPER (*moving to* L *of Margaret*) But from what?

ALICE. I don't know. I don't know if he knows. He's not said one simple, direct word to me since this divorce came up. It's not God who's gone subtle. It's him.

(MORE *enters a little sheepishly down* L *and crosses to* LC)

MORE (*kindly*) Roper, that was harsh: your principles are—(*he cannot resist sending him up*) excellent—the very best quality.

(ROPER *bridles*)

(*Contrite*) No, truly now, your principles are fine. (*He crosses to Alice*) Look, we must make a start on all that food.

MARGARET. Father, can't you be plain with us?

(MORE *looks quickly from Margaret to Alice, then takes Alice's hand*)

MORE. I stand on the wrong side of no statute, and no common law. (*He takes Margaret's hand*) I have not disobeyed my sovereign. I truly believe no man in England is safer than myself. And I want my supper.

(MORE *starts* ALICE *and* MARGARET *up the stairway and goes to* Roper)

We shall need your assistance, Will. There's an excellent Burgundy —if your principles permit.

ROPER. They don't, sir.

MORE. Well, have some water in it.

ROPER. Just the water, sir.

MORE. My poor boy. (*He turns and goes up the stairway*)

(ROPER *follows More*)

ALICE (*stopping half-way up the stairway; as one who will be answered*) Why does Cromwell collect information about you?

MORE. I'm a prominent figure. Someone somewhere's collecting information about Cromwell. Now, no more shirking; we must make a start. (*He shepherds Roper up the stairway*) There's a stuffed swan, if you please.

(ALICE *and* MARGARET *exit at the top of the stairway*)

Will—I'd trust *you* with my life. But not your principles.

(MORE *and* ROPER *ascend the stairway*)

You see, we speak of being anchored to our principles. But if the weather turns nasty you up with an anchor and let it down where there's less wind, and the fishing's better. And "look", we say, "I'm anchored"—(*he laughs, inviting Roper to laugh with him*) "to my principles".

(MORE *and* ROPER *exit at the top of the stairway. The* LIGHTS *change for the Inn Scene. The flower border is raised.*
The COMMON MAN *enters* R *on the rostrum, pulling on a property basket. On top of the basket there is an inn sign "*THE LOYAL SUBJECT*". He hangs the sign on to the pillar up* RC *and inspects it*)

COMMON MAN. "*The Loyal Subject*"—(*to the audience*) a pub. (*He takes a hat and apron from the basket and puts them on*) A publican. (*He takes two horn mugs from the basket, puts them on the ledge at the downstage edge of the rostrum then pushes the basket off* R *on the rostrum*) Oh, he's a deep one that Sir Thomas More.

(*The* COMMON MAN *comes down the steps and exits* R. *He re-enters immediately carrying a lighted candle in a pewter candlestick*)

(*He puts the candlestick on the ledge*) Deep.

(*The* COMMON MAN *exits* R *and re-enters immediately with a barrel*)

(*He sets the barrel in front of the bench* R) It takes a lot of education to get a man as deep as that. (*He puts the mugs and candlestick on the barrel. Straight to the audience*) And a deep nature to begin with, too. (*Deadpan*) The likes of me—(*he flicks around the barrel top with a duster*) can hardly be *expected* to follow the processes of a man like that. (*Slyly*) Can we? (*He inspects the setting*) Right, ready. (*He stands* R *of the steps and calls*) Ready, sir.   **Scene 7**

(CROMWELL *enters* R *on the rostrum and stands on the second step. He carries a wine bottle*)

CROMWELL. Is this a *good* place for a conspiracy, Innkeeper?

PUBLICAN. You asked for a private room, sir.

CROMWELL (*looking around*) Yes. I want one without too many little dark corners.

PUBLICAN. I don't understand you, sir. Just the four corners as you see.

CROMWELL (*sardonically*) You don't understand me.

PUBLICAN. That's right, sir.

CROMWELL. Do you know my name?

PUBLICAN (*promptly*) No, sir.

CROMWELL. Don't be too tactful, Innkeeper.

PUBLICAN. I don't understand, sir.

CROMWELL. When the likes of you *are* too tactful—(*he comes down the steps to* L *of them*) the likes of me begin to wonder who's the fool.

PUBLICAN. I just don't understand you, sir.

(CROMWELL *puts back his head and laughs silently*)

CROMWELL. The master statesmen of us all. "I don't understand." (*He looks at the Publican almost with hatred and moves to* L *of him*) All right. Get out. (*He tosses a coin to the Publican*)

(*The* PUBLICAN *catches the coin and exits down* R)

(*He goes on to the rostrum and calls off* R) Come on!

(RICH *enters* R *on the rostrum. He glances at the bottle in Cromwell's hand and remains cautiously by the exit*)

Yes, it may be that I am a little intoxicated. (*He comes from the rostrum and stands above the barrel*) But not with alcohol—with success. And who has a strong head for success? None of us gets enough of it. (*He opens the bottle*) Except kings. And they're born drunk.

RICH. Success? What success?

CROMWELL. Guess.

RICH (*coming down the steps*) Collector of Revenues for York.
CROMWELL. No, better than that.
RICH. High Constable?
CROMWELL. Better than *that*.
RICH. I didn't know anything else was open. Better than High Constable?

(CROMWELL *straightens up. Despite his tone he is almost shaking with pleasure*)

CROMWELL. Much better. Sir Thomas Paget is retiring. (*He sits on the bench* R, *at the right end of it*)
RICH (*moving to* L *of the barrel*) Secretary to the Council!
CROMWELL. 'Tis astonishing, isn't it?
RICH (*hastily*) Oh, no—I mean—one sees, it's logical.
CROMWELL. No ceremony, no courtship. Be seated.

(RICH *sits* L *of Cromwell on the bench*)

As His Majesty would say.

(RICH *laughs nervously and involuntarily glances around*)

Yes; see how I trust you.
RICH. Oh, I would never repeat or report a thing like that.
CROMWELL. What kind of thing would you repeat or report?
RICH. Well, nothing said in friendship—may I say "friendship"?
CROMWELL (*pouring the wine*) If you like. D'you believe that—that you would never repeat or report anything et cetera? (*He puts the bottle on the floor* R *of the bench*)
RICH. Yes.
CROMWELL. No, but seriously.
RICH. Why, yes.
CROMWELL (*not sinisterly, but rather as a kindly teacher with a promising pupil*) Rich; seriously.
RICH (*after a pause; bitterly*) It would depend what I was offered.
CROMWELL. Don't say it just to please me.
RICH. It's true. It would depend what I was offered.
CROMWELL (*patting Rich's arm*) Everyone knows it; not many people can say it. (*He hands a mug of wine to Rich*) Well, congratulations.
RICH (*suspiciously*) On what?
CROMWELL. I think you'd made a good Collector of Revenues for York Diocese.
RICH (*gripping on to himself*) Is it in your gift?
CROMWELL. Effectively.
RICH (*with conscious cynicism*) What do I have to do for it?
CROMWELL. Nothing. It isn't like that, Rich. There are no rules. With reward and penalties—so much wickedness purchases so much worldly prospering . . . (*He breaks off, suddenly struck*) Are you sure you're not religious?
RICH. Almost sure.

CROMWELL. Get sure. (*He rises and moves down* R) No, it's not like that, it's much more a matter of convenience, administrative convenience. (*He crosses to* L *of the steps*) The normal aim of administration is to keep steady this factor of convenience—as Sir Thomas would agree. (*He crosses down* R) Now, normally when a man wants to change his woman, you let him if it's convenient and prevent him if it's not—(*he crosses to* L *of the steps*) normally indeed it's of so little importance that you leave it to the priests. (*He crosses down* R) But the constant factor is this element of convenience.

RICH. Whose convenience?

CROMWELL. Oh, ours. But everybody's, too. However, in the present instance the man who wants to change his woman is our Sovereign Lord, Harry, by the Grace of God, the Eighth of that name. (*He crosses to* L *of the steps*) Which is a quaint way of saying that if he wants to change his woman he will. So *that* becomes the constant factor. And our job as administrators is to make it as convenient as we can. I say "our job", on the assumption that you'll take this post at York I've offered you? (*He moves to* L *of the bench*)

(RICH *moves along the bench to the right end.* CROMWELL *sits* L *of Rich on the bench*)

RICH. Yes—yes, yes. (*But he seems gloomy*)

CROMWELL (*sharply*) It's a bad sign when people are depressed by their own good fortune.

RICH (*defensively*) I'm not depressed.

CROMWELL. You look depressed.

RICH (*hastily buffooning*) I'm lamenting. I've lost my innocence.

CROMWELL (*dryly*) You lost that some time ago. If you've only just noticed, it can't have been very important to you. (*He reaches across Rich, picks up the bottle and pours more wine*)

RICH (*much struck*) Why, that's true. That's true, it can't.

CROMWELL. Do we experience a sense of release, Master Rich? An unfamiliar freshness in the head, as of open air?

(RICH *and* CROMWELL *drink*)

RICH. Collector of Revenues isn't bad.

CROMWELL. Not bad for a start. Now our present Lord Chancellor—*there's* an innocent man.

RICH (*putting down his mug; indulgently*) The odd thing is—he *is*.

CROMWELL (*looking at Rich with dislike*) Yes, I say he is. (*In a light tone*) The trouble is, his innocence is tangled in this proposition that you can't change your woman without a divorce, and can't have a divorce unless the Pope says so. And although his present Holiness is—judged even by the most liberal standards—a strikingly corrupt old person, yet he still has this word "Pope" attached to him. And from this quite meaningless circumstance I fear some degree of . . .

RICH (*waving his mug; pleased*) Administrative inconvenience.

CROMWELL (*nodding as to a pupil word perfect*) Just so. (*Deadpan*) This goblet that he gave you, how much was it worth?

(RICH *puts down his mug and looks down*)

(*Quite gently*) Come along, Rich, he gave you a silver goblet. How much did you get for it?

RICH. Fifty shillings.

CROMWELL. Could you take me to the shop?

RICH. Yes.

CROMWELL. Where did he get it?

(RICH *is silent*)

It was a gift from a litigant, a woman, wasn't it?

RICH. Yes.

CROMWELL. Which court? Chancery?

(RICH *reaches for the wine bottle*)

(*He restrains Rich*) No, don't get drunk. In which court was this litigant's case?

RICH. Court of Requests.

(CROMWELL *grunts, his face abstracted.* RICH *looks at* CROMWELL *who becoming aware of Rich's regard, smiles*)

CROMWELL. There, that wasn't too painful, was it?

RICH (*laughing a little and a little rueful*) No.

CROMWELL (*rising, stepping forward and spreading his hands*) That's all there is. (*Diabolically*) And you'll find it easier next time.

(RICH *looks up briefly*)

RICH (*unhappily*) What application do they have, these tidbits of information you collect?

CROMWELL. None at all, usually.

RICH (*not looking up; stubbornly*) But sometimes.

CROMWELL. Well, there *are* these men—you know—"upright", "steadfast", men who want themselves to be the constant factor in the situation. Which, of course, they can't be. The situation rolls forward in any case.

RICH (*stubbornly*) So what happens?

CROMWELL (*not liking his tone; coldly*) If they've any sense they get out of the way. (*He goes on to the rostrum*)

RICH. What if they haven't any sense?

CROMWELL (*coldly*) What, none at all? Well then, they're only fit for Heaven. But Sir Thomas has plenty of sense; he could be frightened.

RICH (*looking up; his face nasty*) Don't forget he's an innocent, Master Cromwell.

CROMWELL. I think we'll finish there for tonight. After all, he *is* the Lord Chancellor.

(CROMWELL *exits* R *on the rostrum*)

RICH. You wouldn't find him easy to frighten. (*He calls after Cromwell*) You've mistaken your man this time. He doesn't know how to be frightened.

(CROMWELL *enters* R *on the rostrum and climbs over the ledge to* R *of* RICH *who rises*)

CROMWELL. Doesn't know how to be frightened? Why, then he never put his hand in a candle. Did he? (*He seizes Rich by the wrist and holds his hand in the candle flame*)

(RICH *screeches and darts back, hugging his hand in his armpit and regarding Cromwell with horror*)

RICH. You enjoyed that!

(CROMWELL's *downturned face is amazed*)

(*Triumphantly*) You enjoyed it!

CURTAIN

ACT II

Before the CURTAIN *rises, a loud, single bell rings.* **Scene 1**

When the CURTAIN *rises, the furniture has been reset. The table is angled* LC, *facing down* R. *The armchair is* C, *at the upstage end of the table, facing front. There are small chairs* L *of the table and* L *of the rostrum. The bench* R *has been removed and the stool* RC *is now under the stairway up* RC. MORE *is seated in the armchair* C. ROPER *is standing* L *of the table. He is dressed in black and wears a cross. The* COMMON MAN *enters down* L. *He is carrying a book and his spectacles. He puts on his spectacles. The bell stops.*

COMMON MAN. The interval started early in the year fifteen-thirty and it's now the middle of May, fifteen thirty-two. (*Explanatory*) Two years. During that time a lot of water's flowed under the bridge and one of the things that have come floating along on it is— (*he reads*) "The Church of England, that finest flower of our Island. genius for compromise; that system, peculiar to these shores, the despair of foreign observers, which deflects the torrents of religious passion down the canals of moderation." (*He looks up*) That's very well put. (*He reads*) "Typically, this great effect was achieved not by bloodshed but by simple Act of Parliament. Only an unhappy few were found to set themselves against the current of their times, and in so doing to court disaster. For we are dealing with an age less fastidious than our own. Imprisonment without trial, and even examination under torture, were common practice."

(*The* COMMON MAN *exits down* L. ROPER *paces up and down behind the table.* MORE *watches him. There is a pause*)

MORE. Must you wear those clothes, Will?
ROPER. Yes, I must.
MORE. Why?
ROPER (*crossing to* R *of More*) The time has come for decent men to declare their allegiance.
MORE. And what allegiance are those designed to express?
ROPER. My allegiance to the Church.
MORE. Well, you *look* like a Spaniard.
ROPER (*moving to* L *of the steps*) All credit to Spain, then.
MORE. You wouldn't last six months in Spain. You'd have been burned alive in Spain, during your heretic period.
ROPER (*moving to* R *of More*) I suppose you have the right to remind me of it. (*He points accusingly*) That chain of office that *you* wear is a degradation.
MORE (*glancing down at his chain*) I've told you. If the bishops in

Convocation submitted this morning, I'll take it off. It's no degradation. Great men have worn this.

ROPER. When d'you expect to hear from Canterbury?

MORE. About now. The Archbishop promised me an immediate
message.

ROPER (*pacing down* L) I don't see what difference Convocation
can make. The Church is already a wing of the Palace, is it not?
(*He paces to* L *of the steps*) The King is already its "Supreme Head",
is he not?

MORE. No.

ROPER (*startled*) You are denying the *Act of Supremacy?*

MORE. No, I'm not; the Act states that the King——

ROPER. —is Supreme Head of the Church in England.

MORE. Supreme Head of the Church in England—(*he underlines
the words*) "so far as the law of God allows". How far the law of God
does allow it remains a matter of opinion, since the Act doesn't
state it.

ROPER. A legal quibble.

MORE. Call it what you like, it's there, thank God.

ROPER. Very well. In your opinion, how far does the law of God
allow this?

MORE. I'll keep my opinion to myself, Will.

ROPER (*crossing to* R *of More*) Yes? I'll tell you mine . . .

MORE. Don't! If your opinion's what I think it is, it's High
Treason, Roper.

(MARGARET *enters down the stairway*)

Will you remember you've a wife, now. And may have children.

MARGARET. Why must he remember that?

ROPER (*crossing to* R *of the steps*) To keep myself "discreet".

MARGARET (*moving to* L *of Roper; smiling*) Then I'd rather you
forgot it.

MORE (*unsmiling*) You are either idiots, or children.

(CHAPUYS *enters down the stairway*)

CHAPUYS (*very sonorous*) Or saints, my Lord.

MARGARET. Oh. Father, the Spanish Ambassador has come to
see you.

MORE (*rising*) Your Excellency.

(CHAPUYS *strikes a pose on the rostrum*)

CHAPUYS. Or saints, my lord; or saints.

MORE (*grinning maliciously at Roper*) That's it, of course—saints.
(*With a step towards him*) Roper—turn your head a bit—yes, I think
I do detect a faint radiance. (*Reproachfully*) You should have told us,
Will. (*He moves* C)

CHAPUYS (*crossing to* R *of More*) Come, come, my lord; you, too,
at this time are not free from some suspicion of saintliness.

MORE (*quietly*) I don't like the sound of that, Your Excellency. What do you require of *me?* What, Your Excellency?

(CHAPUYS *crosses down* L *of the table, awkward beneath* MORE's *suddenly keen look*)

CHAPUYS. May I not come simply to pay my respects to the English Socrates—as I see your angelic friend Erasmus calls you. MORE (*wrinkling his nose*) Yes, I'll think of something presently to call Erasmus. (*He checks*) Socrates! I've no taste for hemlock, Your Excellency, if that's what you require.
CHAPUYS (*with a display of horror*) Heaven forbid!
MORE (*dryly*) Amen.
CHAPUYS (*spreading his hands*) Must I require anything? (*Sonorously*) After all, we are brothers in Christ, you and I?
MORE. A characteristic we share with the rest of humanity. You live in Cheapside, Signor? To make contact with a brother in Christ you have only to open your window and empty a chamber-pot. There was no need to come to Chelsea.

(CHAPUYS *titters nervously*)

(*Coldly*) William. The Spanish Ambassador is here on business. Would you mind!

(ROPER *and* MARGARET *go on to the rostrum*)

CHAPUYS (*with unreal protestations*) Oh, no! I protest!
MORE. He is clearly here on business.
CHAPUYS. No; but really, I protest! (*It is no more than a token protest*)

(ROPER *and* MARGARET *go up the stairway*)

(*He calls to Roper and Margaret*) Dominus vobiscum filii mei!
ROPER (*pompously*) Et cum spiritu tuo, Excellencies!

(ROPER *and* MARGARET *exit at the top of the stairs*)

CHAPUYS (*moving to* L *of More; thrillingly*) And how much longer shall we hear that holy language in these shores?
MORE (*alert but poker-faced*) 'Tisn't "holy", Your Excellency; just old.

(CHAPUYS *sits in the armchair* C, *with the air of one coming to brass tacks*)

CHAPUYS. My Lord, I cannot believe you will allow yourself to be associated with the recent actions of King Henry. In respect of Queen Catherine.
MORE. Subjects are associated with the actions of Kings willy nilly.

CHAPUYS. The Lord Chancellor is not an ordinary subject. He bears responsibility—(*he lets the word sink in*)——

(MORE *moves up* C)

—for what is done.

MORE (*agitation beginning to show through*) Have you considered that what has been done badly, might have been done worse, with a different Chancellor?

(CHAPUYS *continues with mounting confidence as* MORE'S *attention is caught*)

CHAPUYS. Believe me, Sir Thomas, your influence in these policies has been much searched for, and where it has been found it has been praised—*but*—there comes a point, does there not?

MORE (*moving above the table*) Yes. (*Agitated*) There does come such a point.

CHAPUYS. When the sufferings of one unfortunate lady swell to an open attack on the religion of an entire country, that point has been passed. Beyond that point, Sir Thomas, one is not merely "compromised", one is in truth corrupted.

MORE (*staring at Chapuys*) What do you want?

CHAPUYS. Rumour has it that if the Church in Convocation has submitted to the King, you will resign.

(MORE *looks down and regains composure*)

MORE (*moving down* L *of the table*) I see. (*Suavely*) Supposing that rumour to be right. Would you approve of that?

CHAPUYS. Approve, applaud, admire.

MORE (*looking down*) Why?

CHAPUYS. Because it would show one man—and that man known to be temperate—unable to go further with this wickedness.

MORE (*still looking down*) And that man known to be Chancellor of England, too.

CHAPUYS. Believe me, my lord, such a signal would be seen . . .

MORE. "Signal"?

CHAPUYS. Yes, my lord; it would be seen and understood.

MORE (*sitting on the chair* L *of the table; now positively silky*) By whom?

CHAPUYS. By half your fellow countrymen.

(MORE *looks up sharply*)

Sir Thomas, I have just returned from Yorkshire and Northumberland, where I have made a tour.

MORE (*softly*) Have you indeed.

CHAPUYS. Things are very different there, my lord. There they are ready.

MORE. For what?

CHAPUYS. Resistance.

(ROPER *enters excitedly down the stairway*)

ROPER. Sir Thomas . . .

(MORE *looks up angrily*)

(*He comes on to the rostrum*) Excuse me, sir—(*he indicates the top of the stairway*) His Grace the Duke of Norfolk.

> (MORE *and* CHAPUYS *rise.*
> NORFOLK *enters at the top of the stairway.*
> ALICE *and* MARGARET *enter* L)

It's all over, sir, they've . . .

NORFOLK (*descending the stairway*) One moment, Roper, I'll do this.

> (ROPER *comes from the rostrum and stands* R *of the steps.* MARGARET *crosses to* L *of the rostrum.* ALICE *stands up* C)

Thomas . . . (*He reaches the rostrum and sees Chapuys*) Oh! (*He stares hostilely at Chapuys*)

CHAPUYS (*crossing and going on to the rostrum*) I was on the point of leaving, Your Grace. Just a personal call. I have been trying —er— to borrow a book—but without success—(*to More*) you're sure you have no copy, my lord? Then I'll leave you. (*He bows*) Gentlemen, ladies. (*He goes up the stairway*)

ROPER (*moving towards More*) Sir Thomas . . .

> (CHAPUYS *stops and listens*)

NORFOLK (*moving to* C) I'll do it, Roper. Convocation's knuckled under, Thomas. They're to pay a fine of a hundred thousand pounds. And—we've severed the connection with Rome.

MORE (*smiling bitterly*) "The connection with Rome" is nice. (*Bitter*) "The connection with Rome."

ROPER (*to Norfolk; looking at More*) Your Grace, this is quite certain, is it?

NORFOLK. Yes.

> (MORE *puts his hand to his chain of office.*
> CHAPUYS *exits at the top of the stairway. The others turn and see him go*)

Funny company, Thomas?

MORE. It's quite unintentional. He doesn't mean to be funny. (*He fumbles with his chain and moves to* L *of Norfolk*) Help me with this.

NORFOLK (*turning away*) Not I.

> (ROPER *takes a step forward*)

ROPER (*subdued*) Shall I, sir?

More. No, thank you, Will. Alice?

Alice (*moving to* L *of More*) Hell's fire—God's blood and body—
no!

(More *listens gravely*)

Sun and moon, Master More, you're taken for a wise man. Is this
wisdom—to betray your ability, abandon practice, forget your
station and your duty to your kin and behave like a printed book?

More. Margaret, will you?

Margaret (*moving to* R *of More*) If you want. (*She removes the chain
then moves above the table and puts the chain on it*)

More. There's my clever girl.

(Alice *sits on the chair* L *of the table*)

Norfolk. Well, Thomas, why? Make me understand—because
I'll tell you now, from where I stand, this looks like cowardice.

More (*excited and angry*) All right, I will. This isn't "Reformation"; this is war against the Church. (*He moves to* L *of Norfolk. Indignantly*) Our King, Norfolk, has declared war on the Pope—
because the Pope will not declare that our Queen is not his wife.

Norfolk. And is she?

More (*cunning*) I'll answer that question for one person only—
the King. Aye, and that in private, too.

Norfolk (*contemptuously*) Man, you're cautious.

More. Yes, cautious. I'm not one of your hawks.

Norfolk (*crossing below More to* L *of him*) All right—we're at war
with the Pope. The Pope's a prince, isn't he?

More. He is.

Norfolk. And a bad one?

More. Bad enough. But the theory is that he's also the Vicar of
God, the descendant of St Peter, our only link with Christ.

Norfolk (*sneering*) A tenuous link.

More. Oh, tenuous indeed.

Norfolk (*to the others*) Does this make sense?

(*The others are silent and look at More*)

You'll forfeit all you've got—which includes the respect of your
country—for a theory?

More (*hotly*) The Apostolic Succession of the Pope is . . . (*He
stops, interested*) Why, it's a theory, yes. You can't see it; can't touch
it; it's a theory. (*Very rapidly but calmly*) But what matters to me is not
whether it's true or not but that I believe it to be true, or rather
not that I *believe* it, but that *I* believe it. I trust I make myself
obscure?

Norfolk. Perfectly.

More. Good. Obscurity's what I have need of now.

Norfolk. Man, you're sick. This isn't Spain, you know.

(MORE *looks at Norfolk then takes him down* C)

MORE (*in a lowered voice*) Have I your word, that what we say here is between us and has no existence beyond these walls?

NORFOLK (*impatiently*) Very well.

MORE (*almost whispering*) And if the King should command you to repeat what I have said?

NORFOLK. I should keep my word to you.

MORE. Then what has become of your oath of obedience to the King?

NORFOLK (*indignantly*) You lay traps for me.

MORE (*now grown calm*) No, I show you the times.

NORFOLK. Why do you insult me with these lawyer's tricks?

MORE. Because I am afraid.

NORFOLK. And here's your answer. The King accepts your resignation very sadly; he is mindful of your goodness and past loyalty and in any matter concerning your honour and welfare he will be your good lord. So much for your fear.

MORE (*flatly*) You will convey my humble gratitude.

NORFOLK. I will. (*He moves to* R *of Alice*) Good day, Alice. (*He crosses to the steps*) I'd rather deal with you than your husband.

MORE (*with a complete change of tone; briskly professional*) Oh, Howard. Signor Chapuys tells me he's just made a "tour" of the North Country. He thinks we shall have trouble there. So do I.

NORFOLK (*moving to* R *of More; stolidly*) Yes? What kind of trouble?

MORE. The Church—the old Church, not the new Church—is very strong up there. I'm serious, Howard. Keep an eye on the Border this next spring, and bear in mind the Old Alliance.

NORFOLK (*looking at More*) We will. We do. (*He moves to the steps*) As for the Spaniard, Thomas, it'll perhaps relieve your mind to know that one of Secretary Cromwell's agents made the tour with him.

MORE. Oh. (*With a flash of jealousy*) Of course, if Master Cromwell has matters in hand . . .

NORFOLK. He has.

MORE. Yes, I can imagine.

NORFOLK. But thanks for the information. (*He ascends the stairway*) It's good to know you still have—some vestige of patriotism.

(NORFOLK *exits at the top of the stairway*)

MORE (*angrily*) That's a remarkably stupid observation, Norfolk.

ALICE. So there's an end of you. What will you do now—sit by the fire and make goslings in the ash?

MORE (*moving down* C) Not at all, Alice. I expect I'll write a bit. (*He woos them with unhappy cheerfulness*) I'll write, I'll read, I'll think. I think I'll learn to fish. I'll play with my grandchildren—when son Roper's done his duty. (*Eagerly*) Alice, shall I teach you to read?

ALICE. No, by God!

MORE. Son Roper, *you're* pleased with me, I hope?

ROPER *(moving to the steps; moved)* Sir, you've made a noble gesture.

MORE *(blankly)* A gesture? *(He turns to face Roper. Eagerly)* It wasn't possible to continue, Will. I was not *able* to continue. I would have if I could. I made no gesture. *(He moves up c and looks apprehensively after Norfolk)* My God, I hope it's understood I make no gesture. *(He turns to Alice)* Alice, you don't think I would do this to you for a gesture? *(He moves to Alice and thumbs his nose)* That's a gesture! *(He jerks up two fingers)* That's a gesture. *(He moves c)* I'm no street acrobat to make gestures. I'm practical.

ROPER *(moving to R of More)* You belittle yourself, sir, this was not practical—*(resonantly)* this was moral.

MORE. Oh, now I understand you, Will. Morality's *not* practical. Morality's a gesture. *(He moves up c)* A complicated gesture learned from books—that's what you say, Alice, isn't it? And you, Meg?

MARGARET. It *is*, for most of us, Father.

MORE. Oh, no, if you're going to plead humility . . . *(He moves down c)* Oh, you're cruel. I have a cruel family.

ALICE. Yes, you can fit the cap on anyone you want, I know that well enough. If there's cruelty in this house, I know where to look for it.

MARGARET *(moving down L of the table)* No, Mother . . .

ALICE. Oh, you'd walk on the bottom of the sea and think yourself a crab if he suggested it. *(She rises and crosses to Roper)* And you! You'd dance him to the Tower—you'd dance him to the block. Like David with a harp. Scattering hymn-books in his path. *(She moves to R of More)* Poor silly man, d'you think they'll *leave* you here to learn to fish?

MORE *(looking straight at Alice)* If we govern our tongues they will. Now listen, I have a word to say about that. I have made no statement. I've resigned, that's *all*. On the King's Supremacy, the King's divorce which he'll now grant himself, the marriage he'll then make —have you heard me make a statement?

ALICE. No—and if I'm to lose my rank and fall to housekeeping I want to know the reason; so make a statement now.

MORE. No.

(ALICE exhibits indignation and crosses down LC)

Alice, it's a point of law. Accept it from me, Alice, that in silence is my safety under the law, but my silence must be absolute, it must extend to you.

ALICE. In short, you don't trust us.

MORE *(impatiently)* A man would need to be half-witted not to trust you, but look—*(he moves to R of Alice)* I'm the Lord Chief Justice, I'm Cromwell, I'm the King's head jailer—and I take your hand—*(he takes Alice's hand)* and I clamp it on the Bible, on the Blessed Cross—*(he clamps her hand on his closed fist)* and I say, "Woman, has your husband made a statement on these matters?" Now—on peril of your soul, remember—what's your answer?

ALICE. "No."

MORE. And so it must remain. (*He looks around at their grave faces*) Oh, it's only a life-line, we shan't have to use it but it's comforting to have. No, no, when they find I'm silent they'll ask nothing better than to leave me silent; you'll see.

(*The* STEWARD *enters down* L)

STEWARD. Sir, the household's in the kitchen. They want to know what's happened.

MORE. Oh. Yes. We must speak to them. Alice, they'll mostly have to go, my dear. (*To the Steward*) But not before we've found them places.

ALICE. We can't find places for them all.

MORE. Yes, we can; yes, we can. Tell them so.

ALICE. God's death, it comes on us quickly.

(ALICE, MARGARET *and* ROPER *exit down* L)

MORE. What about you, Matthew? (*He starts to remove his robe*)

(*The* STEWARD *moves to* L *of More and assists with the robe*)

It'll be a smaller household, now, and for you I'm afraid, a smaller wage. Will you stay?

STEWARD. Don't see how I could, then, sir.

MORE. You're a single man.

STEWARD (*awkwardly*) Well, yes, sir, but I mean—I've got my own . . .

MORE (*quickly*) Quite right, why should you? I shall miss you, Matthew.

STEWARD (*with man-to-man jocosity*) No-o-o. You never had much time for *me*, sir. You see through *me*, sir, I know that. (*He almost winks*)

MORE (*taking the robe from the Steward; gently insisting*) I shall miss you, Matthew; I shall miss you.

(MORE *exits down* L. *The* STEWARD *snatches off his hat and hurls it to the floor*)

STEWARD. New, damn me isn't that them all over! (*He broods, face down-turned*) Miss . . . ? He . . . Miss . . . ? *Miss* me? What's *in* me for *him* to miss? (*He suddenly cries out like one who sees danger at his very feet*) Wo-ah! (*He chuckles*) We-e-eyup! (*To the audience*) I nearly fell for it. "Matthew, will you kindly take a cut in your wages?" "No, Sir Thomas, I will not." That's it, and—(*fiercely*) that's all of it. (*He falls to thought again. Resentfully*) All right, so he's down on his luck. (*He crosses to the chair* L *of the rostrum and places it* C) I'm sorry. I don't mind saying that: I'm sorry. Bad luck. (*He moves the armchair and sets it behind the table*) If I'd any good luck to spare he could have some. I wish we could *all* have good luck *all* the time. I wish we had wings. I wish rainwater was beer. (*He removes the linen tablecloth. There is a velour cloth underneath*) But it isn't. (*He tosses the cloth on to the floor beside his hat*) And what with not having wings but walking—on two flat feet—(*he removes his coat and throws it on to the table-cloth*) and your luck and bad luck being just exactly even stevens; and rain being water—don't you complicate the job by putting things in me for me to miss. (*He bundles up the cloth, coat and hat and picks them up. Chuckling*) I did, you know—I nearly fell for it.

(*The* COMMON MAN *exits down* L. *The* LIGHTS *change for the following scene. A shelf is lowered from the flies. On the shelf there are books, a handbell, a globe of the world, an hour-glass, documents, etc.* **Scene 2**

NORFOLK *and* CROMWELL *enter* L. CROMWELL *carries a portfolio*)

NORFOLK (*crossing to the chair* c) But he makes no noise, Mr Secretary; he's silent—why not leave him silent?

CROMWELL (*sitting in the armchair behind the table; patiently*) Not being a man of letters, Your Grace, you perhaps don't realize the extent of his reputation. This "silence" of his is bellowing up and down Europe. Now, may I recapitulate. He reported the Spaniard's conversation to you, informed on the Spaniard's tour of the North Country, warned against a possible rebellion there.

NORFOLK. He did.

CROMWELL. We may say then, that he showed himself hostile to the hopes of Spain.

NORFOLK. That's what I *say*.

CROMWELL (*patiently*) Bear with me, Your Grace. Now, if he opposes Spain, he supports us. Well, surely that follows? (*Sarcastically*) Or do you see some third alternative?

NORFOLK. No, no, that's the line-up all right. (*He stands above the chair* c) And I may say Thomas More . . .

CROMWELL. Thomas More will line up on the right side.

NORFOLK. Yes. Yes. Crank he may be, traitor he is not.

CROMWELL (*spreading his hands*) And with a little pressure, he can be got to say so. And that's all we need—a brief declaration of his loyalty to the present administration.

NORFOLK (*moving to* L *of the chair* c) I still say let sleeping dogs lie.

CROMWELL (*heavily*) The King does not agree with you.

(NORFOLK *glances at Cromwell, flickers, but then rallies*)

NORFOLK. What kind of "pressure" d'you think you can bring to bear?

CROMWELL (*opening his portfolio*) I have evidence that Sir Thomas, during the period of his judicature, accepted bribes.

NORFOLK (*with a step towards Cromwell; incredulously*) What! Goddammit, he was the only judge since Cato who *didn't* accept bribes.

(*He moves to the chair* C *and sits*) When was there last a Chancellor whose possessions after three years in office totalled one hundred pounds and a gold chain?

(CROMWELL *takes a handbell from the shelf and rings it*)

CROMWELL (*calling*) Richard. (*He turns to Norfolk*) It is, as you imply, common practice, but a practice may be common and remain an offence; this offence could send a man to the Tower.

NORFOLK (*contemptuously*) I don't believe it.

(RICH *and a* WOMAN *enter* L. *The* WOMAN *is in her middle fifties. She is self-opinionated, self-righteous, selfish and indignant.* RICH *has acquired self-importance. He motions the* WOMAN *to* R *of Norfolk*)

CROMWELL. Ah, Richard. (*He indicates the chair* L *of the table*)

(RICH *moves to the chair* L *of the table*)

You know His Grace, of course.

RICH (*with respectful affability*) Indeed yes, we're *old* friends.

NORFOLK (*snubbing savagely*) Used to look after my books or something, didn't you?

(RICH *sits* L *of the table*)

CROMWELL (*clicking his fingers at the Woman*) Come here.

(*The* WOMAN *moves to* R *of the table*)

This woman's name is Catherine Anger; she comes from Lincoln. And she put a case in the Court of Requests in . . . (*He consults his papers*)

WOMAN. A property case, it was.

CROMWELL. Be quiet! A property case in the Court of Requests in April, fifteen twenty-six.

WOMAN. And got a wicked false judgement.

CROMWELL. And got an impeccably correct judgement from our friend Sir Thomas.

WOMAN. No, sir, it was not.

CROMWELL. We're not concerned with the judgement but the gift you gave the judge. Tell this gentleman about that. The judgement, for what it's worth, was the right one.

WOMAN. No, sir.

(CROMWELL *looks at the Woman*)

(*She hastily addresses Norfolk*) I sent him a cup, sir; an Italian silver cup I bought in Lincoln for a hundred shillings.

NORFOLK. Did Sir Thomas accept this cup?

WOMAN. I sent it.

CROMWELL. He did accept it, we can corroborate that. (*To the Woman*) You can go.

(*The* Woman *opens her mouth to speak*)

Go!

(*The* Woman *exits* L)

Norfolk (*scornfully*) Is that your witness?

Cromwell. No; by an odd coincidence this cup later came into the hands of Master Rich, here.

Norfolk. How?

Rich. He gave it to me.

Norfolk (*brutally*) Can you corroborate that?

Cromwell. I have a fellow outside who can; he was More's steward at that time. Shall I call him?

Norfolk. Don't bother, I know him. When did Sir Thomas give you this thing?

Rich. I don't exactly remember.

Norfolk. Well, make an effort. Wait! I can tell you. I can tell you—(*he rises and moves above the table*) it was that spring—it was that evening we were there together. You had a cup with you when we left; was that it?

(Rich *looks to* Cromwell *for guidance but gets none*)

Rich. It may have been.

Norfolk. Did he often give you cups?

Rich. I don't suppose so, Your Grace.

Norfolk. That was it, then. (*With new realization*) And it was April. The April of 'twenty-six. The very month that cow first put her case before him. (*He moves below the chair* C. *Triumphantly*) In other words, the moment he knew it was a bribe, he got rid of it.

(Cromwell *rises and crosses below the table to* RC)

Cromwell (*nodding judicially*) The facts will bear that interpretation, I suppose.

Norfolk. Oh, this is a horse that won't run, Master Secretary.

Cromwell. Just a trial canter, Your Grace. We'll find something better.

(Norfolk *moves to* L *of Cromwell*)

Norfolk (*between bullying and plea*) Look here, Cromwell, I want no part in this.

Cromwell. You have no choice.

Norfolk. What's that you say?

Cromwell. The King particularly wishes you to be active in the matter.

Norfolk (*winded*) He has not told me that.

Cromwell (*politely*) Indeed? He told me.

Norfolk. But *why?*

CROMWELL. We feel that, since you are known to have been a friend of More's, your participation will show that there is nothing in the nature of a "persecution", but only the strict processes of law. As indeed you've just demonstrated. (*He crosses to the table*) I'll tell the King of your loyalty to your friend. (*He turns to face Norfolk*) If you like, I'll tell him that you—(*he looks away*) "want no part of it", too.

NORFOLK (*furiously*) Are you threatening me, Cromwell?

CROMWELL (*facing Norfolk*) My *dear* Norfolk. This isn't Spain.

(NORFOLK *stares at Cromwell for a moment then turns abruptly and exits down* R. CROMWELL *turns a look of glacial coldness upon Rich*)

RICH (*rising*) I'm sorry, Secretary, I'd forgotten he was there that night.

(CROMWELL *scrutinizes Rich dispassionately*)

CROMWELL. You must try to remember these things.

RICH. Secretary, I'm sincerely . . .

(CROMWELL *dismisses the topic with a wave and turns to look after Norfolk*)

CROMWELL. Not such a fool as he looks—the Duke.

RICH (*with a Civil Service simper*) That would hardly be possible, Secretary.

CROMWELL (*collecting his papers and putting them in his portfolio; briskly*) Sir Thomas is going to be a slippery fish, Richard; we need a net with a finer mesh.

RICH (*moving behind the table*) Yes, Secretary.

CROMWELL. We'll weave one for him, shall we, you and I?

RICH (*uncertainly*) I'm only anxious to do what is correct, Secretary.

CROMWELL (*smiling at him*) Yes, Richard, I know. (*Straight-faced*) You're absolutely right, it must be done by law. It's just a matter of finding the right law. Or making one. (*He crosses down* L) Bring my papers, will you?

(CROMWELL *exits down* L.
The STEWARD *enters* L)

STEWARD (*standing above the table*) Could we have a word now, sir?

RICH. We don't require you after all, Matthew.

STEWARD. No, sir, but about . . .

RICH. Oh, yes. Well, I begin to need a steward, certainly; my household is expanding. (*Sharply*) But as I remember, Matthew, your attitude to me was sometimes—(*shrilly*) disrespectful.

STEWARD (*with humble dignity*) Oh. Oh, I must contradict you there, sir; that's your imagination. In those days, sir, you still had your way to make. And a gentleman in that position often imagines these things. Then when he's risen to his proper level, sir, he stops thinking about it. (*As one offering tangible proof*) Well—I don't think you find people "disrespectful" nowadays, do you, sir?

RICH. There may be something in that. (*He indicates the portfolio*) Bring my papers.

(RICH *turns and exits down* L. *The* STEWARD *picks up the portfolio and moves down* L.

RICH *re-enters down* L *and anxiously scans the Steward's face for signs of impudence*)

I'll permit no breath of insolence.

STEWARD (*the very idea is shocking*) I should hope not, sir.

(RICH *exits down* L)

Oh, I can manage this one. He's just my size. (*He folds the front of the table-cloth back on to the top of the table and turns the chair* C *with his foot to face front*) Sir Thomas More's again.

(*The* LIGHTS *change so that the setting looks drab and chilly. The shelf is raised*)

Gone down a bit.

(*The* COMMON MAN *exits down* L.   **Scene 3**
CHAPUYS *and the* ATTENDANT *enter* L *and cross to* C.
ALICE *enters* R *on the rostrum. She wears a big, coarse apron over her dress*)

ALICE. My husband is coming down, Your Excellency.

CHAPUYS. Thank you, madam.

ALICE. And I beg you to be gone before he does.

CHAPUYS (*patiently*) Madam, I have a Royal Commission to perform.

ALICE. Aye. So you said.

(ALICE *exits* R *on the rostrum*)

CHAPUYS. For sheer barbarity, commend me to a good-hearted Englishwoman of a certain class.

ATTENDANT. It's very cold, Excellency.

CHAPUYS. I remember when these rooms were warm enough.

ATTENDANT. "Thus it is to incur the enmity of a prince."

CHAPUYS. Yes, he is a good man.

ATTENDANT. Yes, Excellency, I like Sir Thomas very much.

CHAPUYS. Carefully, carefully!

ATTENDANT. But it's uncomfortable dealing with him.

CHAPUYS. Goodness presents its own difficulties. Attend and learn now.

ATTENDANT. Excellency . . .

CHAPUYS. Well?
ATTENDANT. Excellency, is he really for us?
CHAPUYS. He's opposed to Cromwell. He's shown that, I think.
ATTENDANT. Yes, Excellency, but . . .
CHAPUYS. If he's opposed to Cromwell, he's for us. There's no third alternative.
ATTENDANT. I suppose not, Excellency.
CHAPUYS. I wish your mother had chosen some other career for you, you've no political sense whatever. (*He glances off* R) Ssh!

(MORE *enters* R *on the rostrum. His clothes match the atmosphere of the room and he moves rather more deliberately than before*)

MORE (*moving to the bottom of the steps*) Is this another "personal" visit, Chapuys, or is it official?
CHAPUYS. It falls between the two, Sir Thomas.
MORE. Official, then.
CHAPUYS (*taking out a letter*) No, I have a personal letter for you.
MORE. From whom?
CHAPUYS (*holding out the letter*) From the King of Spain.

(MORE *puts his hands behind his back*)

You will take it?
MORE. I will not lay a finger on it.
CHAPUYS. It is in no way an affair of State. It expresses my master's admiration for the stand which you have taken over the so-called divorce of Queen Catherine.
MORE (*crossing to* LC) I have taken no stand.
CHAPUYS. But your views, Sir Thomas, are well known . . .
MORE. My views are much guessed at.
CHAPUYS (*proffering the letter*) Then . . . ?
MORE (*irritably*) Oh, come, sir, could you undertake to convince —(*grimly*) King Harry that this letter is "in no way an affair of State"?
CHAPUYS (*crossing to* R *of More*) My dear Sir Thomas, I have taken extreme precautions. I came here very much incognito. (*With a self-indulgent chuckle*) Very nearly in disguise.
MORE. You misunderstand me. It is not a matter of your precautions but my duty; which would be to take this letter immediately to the King.
CHAPUYS (*flabbergasted*) But, Sir Thomas, your views . . .
MORE. Are well known, you say. It seems my loyalty is less so.

(MARGARET *enters down* R *and crosses to* RC. *She carries a huge bundle of bracken*)

MARGARET. Look, Father. (*She dumps the bracken on the ground* RC) Will's getting more.
MORE. Oh, well done! (*This is not whimsy. They are cold and their*

interest in fuel is serious) Is it dry? (*He crosses to the bracken and feels it expertly*) Oh, *it is*.

(CHAPUYS *stares*)

(*He sees Chapuys staring and laughs*) It's bracken, Your Excellency. We burn it.

(ALICE *enters* R *on the rostrum*)

(*He indicates the bracken*) Alice, look at this.

ALICE (*eyeing Chapuys*) Aye.

MORE (*moving to* R *of Chapuys*) May I . . . ? (*He takes the letter and displays it to Alice and Margaret*) This is a letter from the King of Spain; I want you to see it's not been opened. I have declined it. You see the seal has not been broken? (*He returns the letter to Chapuys*) I wish I could ask you to stay, Your Excellency—the bracken fire is a luxury.

CHAPUYS (*smiling coldly*) One I must forego. (*He bows. To the Attendant*) Come. (*He crosses to* L, *stops and turns*)

(*The* ATTENDANT *crosses above the table to* L)

(*To More*) May I say I am sure my master's admiration will not be diminished. (*He bows*)

MORE. I am gratified. (*He bows*)

(ALICE *and* MARGARET *curtsy*)

CHAPUYS (*aside to the Attendant*) The man's utterly unreliable.

(CHAPUYS *and the* ATTENDANT *exit* L. *There is a short silence.* ALICE *moves down* RC)

ALICE (*kicking the bundle of bracken*) "Luxury." (*She sits wearily on the bundle*)

MORE. Well, it's a luxury while it lasts. (*He moves to the foot of the steps*) There's not much sport in it for you, is there?

(ALICE *neither answers nor looks at More from the depths of her fatigue*)

(*After a moment's hesitation, he braces himself*) Alice, the money from the Bishops—I can't take it. I wish—oh, Heaven, how I wish I could. But I can't.

ALICE (*as one who has ceased to expect anything*) I didn't think you would.

MORE (*reproachfully*) Alice, there *are* reasons.

ALICE. We couldn't come so deep into your confidence as to *know* these reasons why a man in poverty can't take four thousand pounds?

MORE (*gently but very firmly*) Alice, this isn't poverty.

ALICE. D'you know what we shall eat tonight?

MORE (*trying for a smile*) Yes, parsnips.

ALICE. Yes, parsnips and stinking mutton. (*Straight at him*) For a knight's lady.

MORE (*pleading*) But at the worst, we could be beggars, and still keep company, and be merry together.

ALICE (*bitterly*) Merry!

MORE (*sternly*) Aye, merry!

MARGARET (*putting her arm around Alice*) *I* think you should take that money.

MORE (*sitting on the steps*) Oh, don't you see? If I'm paid by the Church for my writings . . .

ALICE. This has nothing to do with your writings. This was charity pure and simple. Collected from the clergy high and low.

MORE. It would *appear* as payment.

ALICE. You're not a man who deals in appearances.

MORE (*fervently*) Oh, am I not though. (*Calmly*) If the King takes this matter any further, with me or with the Church, it will be very bad, if I even appear to have been in the pay of the Church.

ALICE (*sharply*) Bad?

MORE. If you will have it—dangerous.

MARGARET. But you don't write against the King.

MORE. I write. (*He rises and crosses to c*) And that's enough in times like these.

ALICE. You said there *was* no danger.

MORE. I don't think there is. And I don't want there to be.

(ROPER *enters* R *on the rostrum. He carries a sickle*)

ROPER (*steadily*) There's a gentleman here from Hampton Court.

(ALICE *rises*)

You are to go before Secretary Cromwell. To answer certain charges.

(ALICE *and* MARGARET, *appalled, turn to More*)

MORE (*after a silence; rubbing his nose*) Well, that's all right. We expected that. (*He is not very convincing*) When?

(*The lighting changes, darkness gathering on the others, leaving* MORE *isolated in the light, out of which he answers them in the shadows*)

ROPER. Now.

ALICE (*exhibiting distress*) Ah!

MORE. That means nothing, Alice; that's just technique. Well, I suppose "now" means now.

MARGARET (*moving to More*) Can I come with you?

MORE. Why? No. I'll be back for dinner. I'll bring Cromwell to dinner, shall I? It'd serve him right.

MARGARET (*backing up* c) Oh, Father, don't be witty.

(MARGARET *exits* L)

MORE. Why not? Wit's what's in question.

ROPER (*quietly*) While we are witty, the Devil may enter us unawares.

(ROPER *exits* R *on the rostrum*)

MORE. He's not the Devil, son Roper, he's a lawyer. And my case is watertight.

ALICE. They say he's a very penetrating lawyer.

(ALICE *picks up the bracken and exits down* R)

MORE. What, Cromwell? Pooh, he's a pragmatist—and that's the only resemblance he has to the Devil, son Roper; a pragmatist, the merest plumber.

(*The* LIGHTS *come up for Scene 4. The shelf is lowered from the flies.*

Scene 4

CROMWELL *bustles in down the stairway carrying his portfolio.*

RICH *enters* L, *carrying a portfolio, a small book, a pewter inkwell and a quill. He sits* L *of the table*)

CROMWELL (*moving to* R *of the table*) I'm sorry to invite you here at such short notice, Sir Thomas. (*He puts his portfolio on the table*) Good of you to come. Will you take a seat?

(MORE *sits in the chair* C)

I think you know Master Rich?

MORE. Indeed yes, we're old friends. That's a nice gown you have, Richard.

CROMWELL. Master Rich will make a record of our conversation.

MORE. Good of you to tell me, Master Secretary.

(CROMWELL *laughs appreciatively and moves to* L *of More*)

CROMWELL. Believe me, Sir Thomas—no, that's asking too much —but let me tell you all the same, you have no more sincere admirer than myself.

(RICH *writes*)

Not yet, Rich, not yet.

MORE. If I might hear the charges?

CROMWELL. Charges?

MORE. I understand there are certain charges.

CROMWELL. Some ambiguities of behaviour I should like to clarify—hardly "charges".

MORE. Make a note of that, will you, Master Rich? There are no charges.

CROMWELL (*laughing and shaking his head*) Sir Thomas, Sir Thomas!

(*He sits on the right edge of the table*) You know it amazes me that you, who were once so effective *in* the world, and are now so *much* retired from it, should be opposing yourself to the whole movement of the times? (*He ends on a note of interrogation*)

MORE (*nodding*) It amazes me, too.

(CROMWELL *picks up a document and drops it*)

CROMWELL (*sadly*) The King is not pleased with you.

MORE. I am grieved.

CROMWELL. Yet do you know that even now, if you could bring yourself to agree with the universities, the Bishops, and the Parliament of this realm, there is no honour which the King would be likely to deny you?

MORE (*stonily*) I am well acquainted with His Grace's generosity.

CROMWELL (*coldly*) Very well. (*He rises and nods to Rich*)

(RICH *writes*)

(*He picks up a document and consults it*) You have heard of the so-called "Holy Maid of Kent"—who was executed for prophesying against the King?

MORE. Yes; I knew the poor woman.

CROMWELL (*quickly*) You sympathize with her?

MORE. She was ignorant and misguided; she was a bit mad, I think. And she has paid for her folly. Naturally I sympathize with her.

(CROMWELL *grunts*)

CROMWELL. You admit meeting her. You met her—and yet you did not warn His Majesty of her treason. How was that?

MORE. She spoke no treason. Our conversation was not political.

CROMWELL. My dear More, the woman was notorious. Do you expect me to believe that?

MORE. Happily there were witnesses.

CROMWELL. You wrote a letter to her?

MORE. Yes, I wrote advising her to abstain from meddling with. the affairs of Princes and the State. I have a copy of this letter—also witnessed.

CROMWELL. You have been cautious.

MORE. I like to keep my affairs regular.

(CROMWELL *puts down the document and picks up a small book*)

CROMWELL (*rising and crossing above More to* R *of him*) Sir Thomas, there is a more serious charge.

MORE. Charge?

CROMWELL. For want of a better word. In the May of fifteen twenty-six the King published a book—(*he permits himself a little smile*) a theological work. It was called *A Defence of the Seven Sacraments.*

MORE. Yes. (*Bitterly*) For which he was named "Defender of the Faith", by His Holiness the Pope.

CROMWELL (*moving to* L *of the steps and facing More*) By the Bishop of Rome. Or do you insist on "Pope"?

MORE. No, "Bishop of Rome" if you like. It doesn't alter his authority.

CROMWELL. Thank you, you come to the point very readily. (*He moves to* R *of More*) What *is* that authority? As regards the Church in other parts of Europe; for example, the Church in England. What exactly *is* the Bishop of Rome's authority?

MORE. You will find it very ably set out and defended, Master Secretary, in the King's book.

CROMWELL (*crossing below More to* L *of him*) The book published under the King's name would be more accurate. You wrote this book.

MORE. I wrote no part of it.

CROMWELL. I do not mean you actually held the pen.

MORE. I merely answered to the best of my ability certain questions on canon law which His Majesty put to me. As I was bound to do.

CROMWELL. Do you deny that you *instigated* it?

MORE. It was from first to last the King's own project. This is trivial, Master Cromwell.

CROMWELL (*putting the book on the table*) I should not think so if I were in your place.

MORE. Only two people know the truth of the matter. Myself and the King. And, whatever he may have said to you, he will not give evidence to support this accusation.

CROMWELL (*facing More*) Why not?

MORE. Because evidence is given on oath, and he will not perjure himself. If you don't know that, you don't yet know him.

(CROMWELL *looks viciously at More*)

CROMWELL (*moving behind the table; formally*) Sir Thomas More, is there anything you wish to say to me concerning the King's marriage with Queen Anne?

MORE (*very still*) I understood I was not to be asked that again.

CROMWELL. Evidently you understood wrongly. These charges . . .

MORE (*rising; his anger breaking through*) They are terrors for children, Master Secretary, not for me.

CROMWELL. Then know that the King commands me to charge you in his name with great ingratitude. And to tell you that there never was nor never could be so villainous a servant nor so traitorous a subject as yourself.

MORE. So I am brought here at last.

CROMWELL. Brought? (*He moves and looks over Rich's shoulder at his writing*) You brought yourself to where you stand now.

MORE. Yes. Still, in another sense I was brought.

CROMWELL (*indifferently*) Oh, yes. (*Officially*) You may go home now. For the present.

(MORE *exits down* R. RICH *rises and collects up his papers and writing materials*)

(*He crosses to* LC) I don't like him so well as I did. There's a man who raises the gale and won't come out of harbour.

RICH (*with a covert jeer*) Do you still think you can frighten him?

CROMWELL. No, he's misusing his intelligence.

RICH. What will you do now, then?

CROMWELL (*as to an importunate child*) Oh, be quiet, Rich. We'll do whatever's necessary. The King's a man of conscience and he wants either Sir Thomas More to bless his marriage or Sir Thomas More destroyed. Either will do.

RICH (*shakily*) They seem odd alternatives, Secretary.

CROMWELL. Do they? That's because you're not a man of conscience. If the King destroys a man that's proof to the King that it must have been a bad man, the kind of man a man of conscience *ought* to destroy—and of course a bad man's blessing's not worth having. So either will do.

RICH (*subdued*) I see.

CROMWELL. Oh, there's no going back, Rich. I find we've made ourselves the keepers of this conscience. And it's ravenous.

(CROMWELL *and* RICH *pick up their portfolios and exit down* L. *The shelf is raised. The* LIGHTS *change to the riverside effect.* **Scene 5** *The* COMMON MAN *enters* L, *removes the cloth from the table then exits* L)

MORE (*off* R; *calling*) Boat! Boat!

(MORE *enters* R *on the rostrum and crosses to* LC)

(*To himself*) Oh, come along, it's not as bad as that. (*He calls*) Boat!

(NORFOLK *enters down* R *and stands* R *of the steps*)

(*He turns and crosses to* C. *Pleased*) Howard! I can't get home. They won't bring me a boat.

NORFOLK. Do you blame them?

MORE. Is it as bad as that?

NORFOLK. It's every bit as bad as that.

MORE (*gravely*) Then it's good of you to be seen with me.

NORFOLK (*looking off* R) I followed you.

MORE (*surprised*) Were *you* followed?

NORFOLK. Probably. (*He crosses to* R *of More and faces him*) So listen to what I have to say, you're behaving like a fool. You're behaving like a crank. You're not behaving like a gentleman—all right, that means nothing to you; but what about your friends?

MORE. What about them?

NORFOLK. Goddammit, you're dangerous to know.

MORE. Then don't know me.

NORFOLK. There's something further. You must have realized by now there's a—policy, with regards to you.

(MORE *nods*)

The King is using me in it.

MORE. That's clever. That's Cromwell. You're between the upper and the nether millstones then.

NORFOLK. I am.

MORE. Howard, you must cease to know me.

NORFOLK. I do know you. I wish I didn't, but I do.

MORE. I mean as a friend.

NORFOLK. You *are* my friend.

MORE. I can't relieve you of your obedience to the King, Howard. You must relieve yourself of our friendship. No-one's safe now, and you have a son.

NORFOLK (*crossing below More to* L *of him*) You might as well advise a man to change the colour of his hair. I'm fond of you, and there it is. You're fond of me, and there it is.

MORE. What's to be done then?

NORFOLK (*with deep appeal*) Give in.

MORE (*gently*) I can't, Howard. (*He smiles*) You might as well advise a man to change the colour of his eyes. I can't. Our friendship's more mutable than *that*.

NORFOLK. Oh, that's immutable, is it? The one fixed point in a world of changing friendships is that Thomas More will not give in.

MORE (*urgent to explain*) To me it *has* to be, for that's myself. Affection goes as deep in me as you, I think, but only God is love right through, Howard; and *that's* my *self*.

NORFOLK. And who are you? Goddammit, man, it's disproportionate. *We're* supposed to be the arrogant ones, the proud, splenetic ones—and we've all given in. Why must you stand out? (*He turns away* L. *Quietly and quickly*) You'll break my heart.

MORE (*moved*) We'll do it now, Howard: part, as friends, and meet as strangers. (*He attempts to take Norfolk's hand*)

NORFOLK (*throwing More's hand aside*) Daft, Thomas! Why d'you want to take your friendship from me? For friendship's sake. You say we'll meet as strangers and every word you've said confirms our friendship.

(MORE *takes a last affectionate look at Norfolk*)

MORE. Oh, that can be remedied. (*He crosses to* R *of the steps and turns. In a tone of deliberate insult*) Norfolk, you're a fool.

(NORFOLK *looks startled then smiles and folds his arms*)

NORFOLK. *You* can't place a quarrel; you haven't the style.

MORE. Hear me out. You and your class have "given in"—as you rightly call it—because the religion of this country means nothing to you one way or the other.

NORFOLK. Well, that's a foolish saying for a start; the nobility of England has always been . . .

MORE. The nobility of England, my lord, would have snored through the Sermon on the Mount. But you'll labour like Thomas Aquinas over a rat-dog's pedigree. Now, what's the name of those distorted creatures you're all breeding at the moment?

NORFOLK (*steadily; but roused towards anger by More's tone*) An artificial quarrel's not a quarrel.

MORE (*crossing to R of Norfolk*) Don't deceive yourself, my lord, we've had a quarrel since the day we met, our friendship was but sloth.

NORFOLK. You can be cruel when you've a mind to be; but I've always known that.

MORE. What's the name of those dogs? Marsh mastiffs? Bog beagles?

NORFOLK. Water spaniels.

MORE. And what would you do with a water spaniel that was afraid of water? You'd hang it. Well, as a spaniel is to water, so is a man to his own self. I will not give in because I oppose it—*I* do—not my pride, not my spleen, nor any other of my appetites, but *I* do—*I*. (*He feels Norfolk up and down like an animal*)

MARGARET (*off R in the distance; calling*) Father!

(MORE's *attention is irresistibly caught by the sound of Margaret's voice but he turns back determinedly to Norfolk*)

MORE. Is there no single sinew in the midst of this that serves no appetite of Norfolk's but is, just, Norfolk? There is. Give *that* some exercise, my lord.

MARGARET (*off; nearer*) Father.

NORFOLK (*breathing hard*) Thomas . . .

MORE. Because as you stand, you'll go before your Maker in a very ill condition.

(MARGARET *enters R on the rostrum and stops, amazed at them*)

NORFOLK. Now steady, Thomas.

(MARGARET *watches from the left end of the rostrum*)

MORE. And he'll have to think that somewhere back along your pedigree—a bitch got over the wall.

(NORFOLK *lashes out at* MORE *who ducks and winces.*
    NORFOLK *exits down* L)

MARGARET (*moving to R of More*) Father!

(MORE *straightens up*)

Father, what was that?

MORE (*moving* L) That was Norfolk. (*He looks wistfully after Norfolk*)

(ROPER *enters* R *on the rostrum and crosses to* R *of More*)

ROPER (*excited; almost gleeful*) Do you know, sir? Have you heard?

(MORE, *still looking off, does not reply*)

(*He turns to Margaret*) Have you told him?

MARGARET (*gently*) We've been looking for you, Father.

(MORE *continues to look off* L)

ROPER. There's to be a new Act through Parliament, sir.

MORE (*half turning; half attending*) Act?

ROPER. Yes, sir—about the marriage.

MORE (*indifferently*) Oh. (*He looks off* L)

(ROPER *and* MARGARET *look at one another.* MARGARET *crosses below Roper to* R *of More and puts a hand on his arm*)

MARGARET. Father, by this Act, they're going to administer an oath.

MORE (*turning; instantaneously attending*) An oath! (*He looks from one to the other*) On what compulsion? (*He moves to* R *of Margaret*)

ROPER. It's expected to be treason.

MORE (*very still*) What is the oath?

ROPER (*puzzled*) It's about the marriage, sir.

MORE. But what is the wording?

ROPER. We don't need to know the—(*contemptuously*) wording—we know what it will mean.

MORE. It will mean what the words say. An oath is *made* of words. It may be possible to take it. Or avoid it. (*To Margaret*) Have we a copy of the Bill?

MARGARET. There's one coming out from the city.

MORE. Then let's get home and look at it. (*He crosses down* L) Oh, I've no boat. (*He looks off again after Norfolk*)

MARGARET (*gently*) Father, he tried to hit you.

MORE. I spoke, slightingly, of water spaniels. (*He crosses and stands between Margaret and Roper*) Let's get home. Now listen, Will. And Meg, you know I know you well, you listen, too. God made the *angels* to show Him splendour—as He made animals for innocence and plants for their simplicity. But Man He made to serve Him wittily, in the tangle of his mind. If He suffers us to fall to such a case that there is no scaping, then we may stand to our tackle as best we can, and yes, Will, then we may clamour like champions—if we have the spittle for it. And no doubt it delights God to see splendour where He only looked for complexity. But it's God's part, not our own, to bring ourselves to that extremity. Our natural business lies in escaping—so let's get home and study this Bill.

(MARGARET, MORE *and* ROPER *exit down* R. *The* LIGHTS *change for the following Scene. A "torture rack" is lowered from the flies* C.

The COMMON MAN *enters* R *dragging a prison cage which he sets on the rostrum* R. *He then crosses and exits down* L. *He re-enters pulling on the property basket. He takes a Jailer's jacket from the basket.*   **Scene 6**

COMMON MAN (*putting on the jacket; aggrieved*) Now look! I don't suppose anyone enjoyed it any more than he did. Well, not much more. (*He takes a Jailer's skull-cap from the basket, puts it on, then pushes the basket into the corner down* L) Jailer. (*He shrugs*) The pay scale being what it is they have to take a rather common type of man into the prison service. But it's a job. (*He moves the chair below the table and sets it behind the left end of the table, then moves the chair* C *and places it above the right end of the table. He then goes on to the rostrum and opens the gate of the cage*)

(MORE *enters* R *on the rostrum, goes into the cage, and lies down. He has aged and is pale, but his manner, though wary, is relaxed*)

(*He locks the gate, removes the keys then sits on the bottom step* RC) Bit nearer the knuckle than most, perhaps, but it's a job like any other job.

(CROMWELL, NORFOLK, RICH *and* ARCHBISHOP THOMAS CRANMER *enter* L. CRANMER *is in his late forties. He is sharp-minded and sharp-faced. He treats the Church as a job of administration and theology as a set of devices, for he lacks personal religiosity.* NORFOLK *sits in the centre chair behind the table.* CROMWELL *sits above Norfolk and* CRANMER *sits below Norfolk.* RICH *stands behind them. The* COMMISSION *is bored, tense and jumpy*)

They'd let him out if they could, but for various reasons they can't. (*He twirls the keys*) I'd let him out if I could, but I can't. Not without taking up residence in there myself. And he's in there already, so what'd be the point? You know the old adage? "Better a live rat than a dead lion," and that's about it.

(*A letter descends swiftly* C *from the flies*)

(*He rises, picks up the letter, opens it and reads*) "With reference to the old adage: Thomas Cromwell was found guilty of High Treason and executed on the twenty-eighth of July fifteen-forty. Norfolk was found guilty of High Treason and should have been executed on the twenty-seventh January fifteen forty-seven but on the night of the twenty-sixth January, the King died of syphilis and wasn't able to sign the warrant. Thomas Cranmer, Archbishop of Canterbury" —(*he jerks his thumb towards Cranmer*) that's the other one—"was burned alive on the twenty-first March fifteen fifty-six." (*He is about to conclude but sees a postscript*) Oh. "Richard Rich became a Knight and Solicitor-General, a Baron and Lord Chancellor, and died in his bed." (*He

puts the letter inside his shirt and goes to the door of the cage) So did I.
And so, I hope will all of you. (*He unlocks the door and rouses More*)
MORE (*rousing*) What, again?
JAILER. Sorry, sir.
MORE (*flopping back*) What time is it?
JAILER. One o'clock, sir.
MORE. Oh, this is iniquitous.
JAILER (*anxiously*) Sir.
MORE (*sitting up*) All right. Who's there?
JAILER. The Secretary, the Duke and the Archbishop.
MORE. I'm flattered. (*He stands then clasps a hand to his hip*) Ooh!

(*The* JAILER *comes from the rostrum.* MORE *limps down and stands up* C)

NORFOLK (*looking at More*) A seat for the prisoner.

(*The* JAILER *moves the stool from under the stairway and places it* C.
MORE *sits on the stool*)

(*He rattles off*) This is the Seventh Commission to enquire into the
case of Sir Thomas More, appointed by His Majesty's Council.
Have you anything to say?
MORE. No. (*To the Jailer*) Thank you.

(*The* JAILER *stands* R *of the steps*)

NORFOLK (*sitting back*) Mr Secretary.
CROMWELL. Sir Thomas . . . (*He breaks off*) Do the witnesses
attend?
RICH. Mr Secretary.
JAILER. Sir.
CROMWELL (*to the Jailer*) Nearer.

(*The* JAILER *advances a step or two*)

Come where you can hear.

(*The* JAILER *moves and stands up* C *under the stairway*)

(*He holds up a document*) Sir Thomas, you have seen this document
before?
MORE. Many times.
CROMWELL (*rising and moving to* L *of More*) It is the Act of Succes-
sion. These are the names of those who have sworn to it.
MORE. I have, as you say, seen it before.
CROMWELL. Will you swear to it?
MORE. No.
NORFOLK. Thomas, we must know plainly . . .
CROMWELL (*moving to* R *of the table and throwing down the document*)
Your Grace, *please*.
NORFOLK (*half rising*) Master Cromwell!

(CROMWELL *and* NORFOLK *regard one another in hatred*)

CROMWELL (*resuming his seat*) I beg Your Grace's pardon. (*He sighs and rests his head in his hands*)
NORFOLK. Thomas, we must know plainly whether you recognize the offspring of Queen Anne as heirs to His Majesty.
MORE. The King in Parliament tells me that they are. Of course I recognize them.
NORFOLK. Will you swear that you do?
MORE. Yes.
NORFOLK. Then why won't you swear to the Act?
CROMWELL (*impatiently*) Because there is more than that *in* the Act.
NORFOLK. Is that it?
MORE (*after a pause*) Yes.
NORFOLK. Then we must find out what it is in the Act that he objects to.
CROMWELL. Brilliant!

(NORFOLK *rounds on Cromwell*)

CRANMER (*hastily*) Your Grace—may I try?
NORFOLK. Certainly. *I*'ve no pretension to be an expert, in police work.

(CROMWELL, *during the next speech, straightens up and folds his arms resignedly*)

CRANMER (*fussily clearing his throat*) Sir Thomas, it states in the preamble, that the King's former marriage to the Lady Catherine, was unlawful, she being previously his brother's wife and the—er— "Pope" having no authority to sanction it. (*Gently*) Is that what you deny?

(MORE *is silent*)

Is that what you dispute?

(MORE *is silent*)

Is that what you are not sure of?

(MORE *is silent*)

NORFOLK. Thomas, you insult the King and his Council in the person of the Lord Archbishop?
MORE. I insult no-one. I will not take the oath. I will not tell you why I will not.
NORFOLK. Then your reasons must be treasonable.
MORE. Not "must be"; may be.
NORFOLK. It's a fair assumption.

MORE. The law requires more than an assumption; the law requires a fact.

(CROMWELL *looks at More and away again*)

CRANMER. I cannot judge your legal standing in the case; but until I know the *ground* of your objections, I can only guess your spiritual standing, too.

(MORE *is for a second furiously affronted, then humour overtakes him*)

MORE. If you're willing to guess at that, Your Grace, it should be a small matter to guess my objections.

CROMWELL (*quickly*) You do have objections to the Act?

NORFOLK (*happily*) Well, we know *that*, Cromwell.

MORE. You don't, my lord. You may *suppose* I have objections. All you *know* is that I will not swear to it. From sheer delight to give you trouble, it might be.

NORFOLK. Is it material why you won't?

MORE. It's most material. For refusing to swear, my goods are forfeit and I am condemned to life imprisonment. You cannot lawfully harm me further. But if you were right in supposing I had reasons for refusing and right again in supposing my reasons to be treasonable, the law would let you cut my head off.

NORFOLK (*who has followed with some difficulty*) Oh, yes.

CROMWELL (*in an admiring murmur*) Oh, well done, Sir Thomas. I've been trying to make that clear to His Grace for some time.

(NORFOLK *hardly responds to the insult; his face is gloomy and disgusted*)

NORFOLK. Oh, confound all this! (*With real dignity*) I'm not a scholar, as Master Cromwell never tires of pointing out, and frankly I don't know whether the marriage was lawful or not. But damn it, Thomas, look at those names. You know those men. Can't you do what I did, and come with us, for fellowship?

MORE (*moved*) And when we stand before God, and you are sent to Paradise for doing according to your conscience, and I am damned for not doing according to mine, will you come with me, for fellowship?

CRANMER. So those of us whose names are there are damned, Sir Thomas?

MORE. I don't know, Your Grace. I have no window to look into another man's conscience. I condemn no-one.

CRANMER. Then the matter is capable of question?

MORE. Certainly.

CRANMER. But that you owe obedience to your King is not capable of question. So weigh a doubt against a certainty—and sign.

MORE. Some men think the earth is round, others think it flat; it is a matter capable of question. But if it is flat, will the King's command make it round? And if it is round, will the King's command flatten it? No, I will not sign.

CROMWELL (*leaping up and moving in front of the table; with ceremonial indignation*) Then you have more regard to your own doubt than you have to his command.

MORE. For myself, I have no doubt.

CROMWELL. No doubt of what?

MORE. No doubt of my grounds for refusing this oath. Grounds I will tell to the King alone, and which you, Mr Secretary, will not trick out of me.

NORFOLK. Thomas . . .

MORE. Oh, gentlemen, can't I go to bed?

CROMWELL (*crossing to L of the steps*) You don't seem to appreciate the seriousness of your position.

MORE. I defy anyone to live in that cell for a year and not appreciate the seriousness of his position.

CROMWELL. Yet the State has harsher punishments.

MORE. You threaten like a dockside bully.

CROMWELL. How should I threaten?

MORE. Like a Minister of State, with justice.

CROMWELL (*moving and standing above More*) Oh, justice is what you're threatened with.

MORE. Then I'm not threatened.

NORFOLK. Master Secretary, I think the prisoner may retire as he requests. (*To Cranmer*) Unless you, my lord . . . ?

CRANMER (*pettishly*) No, I see no purpose in prolonging the interview.

NORFOLK. Then good night, Thomas.

(MORE *rises and moves a step towards the table*)

MORE (*hesitantly*) Might I have one or two more books?

CROMWELL. You have books?

MORE. Yes.

CROMWELL (*moving above the table*) I didn't know; you shouldn't have.

(MORE *crosses to the steps, then pauses and turns*)

MORE (*desperately*) May I see my family?

CROMWELL. No.

(MORE *goes on to the rostrum and into the cage*)

(*He moves to the stool*) Jailer!

JAILER (*moving to L of Cromwell*) Sir.

CROMWELL. Have you ever heard the prisoner speak of the King's divorce, or the King's supremacy of the Church, or the King's marriage?

JAILER. No, sir, not a word.

CROMWELL. If he does, you will of course report it to the Lieutenant.

JAILER. Of course, sir.

CROMWELL. You will swear an oath to that effect.

JAILER (*cheerfully*) Certainly, sir.

CROMWELL (*sitting on the stool*) Archbishop?

(CRANMER *rises and lays the cross of his vestment on the table. The* JAILER *crosses to Cranmer*)

CRANMER. Place your left hand on this and raise your right hand —take your hat off.

(*The* JAILER *removes his hat, puts his left hand on the cross and raises his right hand*)

Now, say after me—"I swear by my immortal soul——

(*The* JAILER, *overlapping, repeats the oath with Cranmer*)

—that I will report truly anything said by Sir Thomas More against the King the Council or the State of the Realm. So help me God. Amen."

JAILER (*overlapping*) "So help me God. Amen." (*He crosses to the steps*)

CROMWELL. And there's fifty guineas in it if you do.

JAILER (*looking gravely at Cromwell*) Yes, sir.

CRANMER (*hastily*) That's not to tempt you into perjury, my man.

JAILER. No, sir. (*He crosses to* R *and pauses. To the audience*) Fifty guineas isn't tempting; fifty guineas is alarming. If he'd left it at swearing . . . But fifty—that's serious money. If it's worth that much now it's worth my neck presently. (*Decisively*) I want no part of it. They can sort it out between them. I feel my deafness coming on.

(*The* JAILER *exits down* R)

CROMWELL. Rich.

RICH (*moving above the table*) Secretary?

CROMWELL. Tomorrow morning, remove the prisoner's books.

NORFOLK. Is that necessary?

CROMWELL (*rising and moving up* C; *with suppressed exasperation*) Norfolk! With regards this case, the King is becoming impatient.

NORFOLK. Aye, with you. (*He rises*)

(CRANMER *rises*)

CROMWELL. With all of us. (*He faces the table*) You know the King's impatience, how commodious it is.

(NORFOLK *exits* L.

CRANMER *exits down* L. CROMWELL *broods over the torture rack up* C. RICH *picks up Cromwell's document*)

RICH (*moving towards Cromwell*) Secretary.

CROMWELL (*abstracted*) Yes?

RICH. Sir Redvers Llewellyn has retired.

CROMWELL (*not listening*) Mm?

RICH (*moving to the other end of the rack and facing Cromwell; with some indignation*) The Attorney General for Wales. His post is vacant. You said I might approach you.

CROMWELL (*with contemptuous impatience*) Oh, not *now*. (*He broods*) He must submit, the alternatives are bad. While More's alive the King's conscience breaks into fresh stinking flowers every time he gets from bed. And if I bring about More's death—I plant my own, I think. There's no other good solution. He must submit. (*He whirls the windlass of the rack, producing a startling clatter from the ratchet*)

(RICH *and* CROMWELL *look at each other*)

No; the King will not permit it. (*He crosses down* L) We have to find some gentler way.

(CROMWELL *exits down* L.

RICH *exits* L. *The* LIGHTS *change from night and it becomes morning with cold grey light from off the grey water.*   **Scene 7**

MARGARET, *the* JAILER, ROPER *and* ALICE *enter down the stairway.* MARGARET *carries a basket covered with a napkin.* ROPER *carries a bottle of wine*)

JAILER (*crossing below Margaret to the cage*) Wake up, Sir Thomas! Your family's here!

MORE (*starting up; with a great cry*) Margaret! What's this? You can visit me? (*He thrusts his arms through the bars*) Meg. Meg.

(*The* JAILER *stands aside and* MARGARET *goes to the cage*)

(*Horrified*) For God's sake, Meg, they've not put *you* in here?

JAILER (*reassuringly*) No-o-o, sir. Just a visit; a short one.

MORE (*excitedly*) Jailer, Jailer, let me out of this.

JAILER (*stolidly*) Yes, sir. I'm allowed to let you out.

MORE. Thank you.

(*The* JAILER *unlocks the gate*)

Thank you, thank you. (*He comes out of the cage*)

(MORE *and* MARGARET *regard each other, then she drops into a curtsy. The* JAILER *exits up the stairway*)

MARGARET. Good morning, Father.

MORE (*wrapping her to him; ecstatically*) Oh, good morning—good morning. Good morning, Alice. Good morning, Will.

(ALICE *approaches More and peers at him technically.* ROPER *moves to* R *of the steps*)

ALICE (*almost accusatory*) Husband, how do you do?

MORE (*smiling over Margaret*) As well as need be, Alice. Very happy now. Will?

(ALICE *goes down the steps and crosses down* L *of the table*)

ROPER. This is an awful place.

MORE. Except it's keeping me from you, my dears, it's not so bad. (*He looks around*) Remarkably like any other place.

(MARGARET *crosses to the table, puts the basket on it, then gets the stool and places it* R *of the table*)

ALICE (*looking up critically*) It drips.

MORE. Yes. Too near the river. (*He comes down the steps*)

(ALICE *sits above the left end of the table, her face bitter*)

MARGARET (*unpacking the basket*) We've brought you some things.

(*There is constraint between* MORE *and* MARGARET)

Some cheese.

MORE. Cheese.

MARGARET. And a custard.

MORE. A custard!

MARGARET. And, these other things. (*She does not look at More*)

ROPER (*holding out the bottle*) And a bottle of wine.

MORE. Oh. (*Mischievously*) Is it good, son Roper?

ROPER. I don't know, sir.

MORE (*looking at them; puzzled*) Well.

ROPER (*moving to* R *of More*) Sir, come out. Swear to the Act. Take the oath and come out.

MORE. Is this why they let you come?

ROPER. Yes. Meg's under oath to persuade you.

MORE (*sitting on the stool; coldly*) That was silly, Meg. How did you come to do that?

MARGARET (*crossing to* R *of More*) I wanted to.

MORE (*incredulously*) You want me to swear to the Act of Succession?

MARGARET (*kneeling beside More*) "God more regards the thoughts of the heart than the words of the mouth"—or so you've always told me.

MORE. Yes.

MARGARET. Then say the words of the oath. and in your heart think otherwise.

MORE. What is an oath, then, but words that we say to God?

MARGARET. That's very neat.

MORE. D'you mean it isn't true?

MARGARET. No, it's true.

MORE (*severely*) Then it's poor argument to call it "neat", Meg.

(*More gently, anxious to convince*) When a man takes an oath, Meg, he's holding his own self in his own hands. (*He shows her, cupping his hands*) Like water. And if he opens his fingers then—he needn't hope to find himself again. Some men aren't capable of this, but I'd be loth to think your father one of them.

MARGARET (*nodding gravely*) So should I.

MORE (*rising; attempting to end it*) Then . . .

MARGARET. There's something else that I've been thinking.

MORE (*pleading*) Oh, Meg . . .

MARGARET (*ruthlessly*) In any State that was half good, you would be raised up high—not here—for what you've done already.

MORE. All right.

MARGARET. It's not your fault the State's three-quarters bad.

MORE. No.

MARGARET. Then if you elect to suffer for it, you elect yourself a hero.

(MORE *smiles a little. He cannot help being proud of Margaret*)

MORE. That's very neat. But look. (*He thinks as he speaks, but with mounting certainty*) If we lived in a State where virtue was profitable, common sense would make us good, and greed would make us saintly. And we'd live like animals or angels in the happy land that *needs* no heroes. But since in fact we see that avarice, anger, envy, pride, sloth, lust and stupidity commonly profit far beyond humility, chastity, fortitude, justice and thought, and have to choose, to be human at all—why then perhaps we *must* stand fast a little—even at the risk of being heroes.

MARGARET (*emotionally*) But in reason. Haven't you done as much as God can reasonably *want?*

MORE. Well—finally—it isn't a matter of reason; it's a matter of love.

ALICE (*hostile*) You're content then, to be shut up here with mice and rats when you might be home with us.

MORE (*flinching*) Content? If they'd open a crack that wide—(*he gestures with thumb and finger*) I'd be through it like a bird. (*To Margaret*) Well, has Eve run out of apples?

MARGARET (*rising*) I've not yet told you what the house is like, without you.

MORE. Don't, Meg.

MARGARET. What we do in the evenings, now that you're not there.

MORE. Meg, have done.

MARGARET. We sit in the dark because we've no candles. And we've no talk because we're wondering what they're doing to you here.

MORE. The King's more merciful than you, he doesn't use the rack.

(*The* JAILER *enters down the stairway*)

JAILER. Two minutes to go, sir. I thought you'd like to know.
MORE. Two minutes. (*He moves up* C)
JAILER. Till seven o'clock, sir. Sorry. Two minutes.

(*The* JAILER *exits up the stairway*)

MORE. Jailer . . . ! (*He seizes Roper by the arm*) Will—go to him, talk to him, keep him occupied. (*He propels Roper towards the steps*)
ROPER. How, sir?
MORE. Anyhow. Have you got any money?
ROPER (*eagerly*) Yes. (*He goes up the steps*)
MORE. No, don't try and bribe him. Let him play for it; he's got a pair of dice. And talk to him, you understand. (*He crosses to the table, picks up the bottle of wine and hands it to Roper*) And take this—and mind you share it—do it properly, Will.

(ROPER *nods vigorously and exits up the stairway*)

(*He moves to* R *of the table*) Now, listen, you must leave the country. All of you must leave the country.
MARGARET (*moving to* R *of More*) And leave you here?
MORE. It makes no difference, Meg; they won't let you see me again. (*Breathlessly; a prepared speech under pressure*) You must all go on the same day, but not on the same boat; different boats from different ports.
MARGARET. After the trial, then.
MORE. There's to be no trial, they have no case. Do this for me, I beseech you?
MARGARET. Yes. (*She moves up* C)
MORE. Alice?

(ALICE *turns her back*)

ALICE. I command it.
ALICE (*harshly*) Right.
MORE (*sitting on the stool and looking into the basket*) Oh, this is splendid; I know who packed this.
ALICE (*harshly*) I packed it.
MORE. Yes. (*He eats a morsel*) You still make superlative custard, Alice.
ALICE. Do I?
MORE. That's a nice dress you have on.
ALICE. It's my cooking dress.
MORE. It's very nice, anyway. Nice colour.
ALICE (*turning to him; quietly*) By God, you think very little of me. (*With mounting bitterness*) I know I'm a fool. But I'm no such fool as at this time to be lamenting for my dresses. Or to relish complimenting me on my custard.

(MORE *regards Alice with frozen attention and nods once or twice*)

MORE. I am well rebuked. (*He holds out his hands*) Al . . .
ALICE. No. (*She remains where she is, glaring at him*)
MORE (*he is in great fear of her*) I am faint when I think of the worst that they may do to me. But worse than that would be to go, will you not understand why I go.
ALICE. I don't.
MORE (*just hanging on to his self-possession*) Alice, if you can tell me that you understand, I think I can make a good death, if I have to.
ALICE. Your death's no "good" to me.
MORE. Alice, you must tell me that you understand.
ALICE. I don't. (*She throws it straight at his head*) I don't believe this had to happen.
MORE (*his face drawn*) If you say that, Alice, I don't see how I'm to face it.
ALICE. It's the truth.
MORE (*rising; with a gasp*) You're an honest woman.
ALICE. Much good may it do me. I'll tell you what I'm afraid of—that when you've gone, I shall hate you for it.
MORE (*turning away* C; *his face working*) Well, you mustn't, Alice, that's all.

(ALICE *rises and crosses swiftly to* MORE, *who turns. They clasp each other fiercely*)

ALICE. S-s-sh! As for understanding, I understand you're the best man I have ever met or am ever likely to, and if you go, well Heaven knows why, I suppose—though Heaven's my witness, Heaven's kept deadly quiet about it. And if anyone wants my opinion of the King and his Council, they only have to ask for it.
MORE. Why, it's a lion I married, a lion. A lion! A lion! (*He breaks from Alice and sits on the stool*) Say what you may, this custard's good. It's very good.

(ALICE *moves behind More and* MARGARET *moves to* R *of him, to comfort him.*
    The JAILER *and* ROPER *enter down the stairway*)

JAILER (*as he enters; to Roper*) It's no good, sir. I know what you're up to. And it can't be done.

(MARGARET *moves* C. MORE *packs the food in the basket*)

ROPER (*disgusted*) Another minute, man.
JAILER (*half-way down the stairway; to More*) Sorry, sir. Time's up.
ROPER (*gripping the Jailer's shoulder from behind*) For pity's sake!
JAILER (*shaking him off*) Now, don't do that, sir. (*He descends the stairway*) Sir Thomas, the ladies will have to go now.

(ROPER *descends the stairway*)

MORE. You said seven o'clock.

JAILER. It's seven, now. You must understand my position, sir.

MORE (*rising*) But one more minute.

MARGARET. Only a little while—give us a little while.

JAILER (*reprovingly*) Now, miss, you don't want to get me into trouble.

ALICE (*moving* c) Do as you're told. Be off at once!

(*The first stroke of seven is heard on a heavy, deliberate bell, which continues, reducing what follows to a babble*)

JAILER (*taking Margaret firmly by the upper arm*) Now come along, miss; you'll get your father into trouble as well as me.

(ROPER *grabs the Jailer*)

Are you obstructing me, sir?

(MARGARET *embraces More, then runs up the stairway and exits.*
ROPER *follows her off*)

(*He moves between Alice and More and takes Alice gingerly by the arm*)
Now, my lady, no trouble.

ALICE (*throwing him off*) Don't put your muddy hand on me. (*She backs to the steps*)

JAILER (*following Alice*) Am I to call the guard, then? Then come on!

(ALICE *backs up the steps. The* JAILER *follows her*)

MORE (*crossing to the steps*) For God's sake, man, we're saying good-bye.

(ALICE *starts to ascend the stairway*)

JAILER (*going on to the rostrum*) You don't know what you're asking, sir. You don't know how you're watched.

ALICE (*half-way up the stairway*) Filthy, stinking, gutter-bred turnkey.

JAILER (*following Alice up the stairway*) Call me what you like, ma'am; you've got to go.

ALICE. I'll see you suffer for this.

JAILER. You're doing your husband no good.

MORE. Alice—good-bye, my love.

(*The last stroke of seven sounds.*
ALICE *raises her hand, turns and exits with considerable dignity at the top of the stairway*)

JAILER (*at the top of the stairway; reasonably*) You understand my position, sir, there's nothing I can do; I'm a plain, simple man and just want to keep out of trouble.

MORE (*crying out passionately*) Oh, sweet Jesus! These plain, simple men! (*He crouches on the bottom step*)

(*A portentous and heraldic fanfare is heard. The* LIGHTS *change for the Trial Scene. Five large Royal Coats of Arms are lowered from the flies. Two drop in too low. Two are too high.*

The JAILER *descends the stairway, removes his jailer's coat and cap, puts them in the cage and pushes the cage off* R. *He re-enters, collects the upstage chair and exits with it* L. *He re-enters and moves the centre chair to* C. MORE *rises and sits in the chair* C.

CROMWELL *enters down* R, *carrying a "clearing-pole" and adjusts the Coats of Arms. He pushes the first up to its dead with the pole, brings down two, moves to dead the next and is about to push it up but it goes up to its dead just before the pole touches it.*

The COMMON MAN *meanwhile pushes the table up* C, *under the stairway then picks up the stool and Margaret's basket and exits with them* L. *He re-enters and takes the downstage chair off* L. *He re-enters with two short benches which he sets* L. *There are six poles attached vertically to each bench. He takes several hats from the property basket and puts them on the poles, these indicating the Jurymen. He takes a portfolio of documents from the basket and puts it on the table. He then crosses, exits* R *on the rostrum and re-enters with a throne chair, places it on the rostrum at the left end, exits again and re-enters with a second throne chair which he places* R *of the first. Large heraldic banners are lowered from the flies up* C. *They are narrow panels, scarlet and bearing the monogram "H R VIII".* CROMWELL *hands the clearing-pole to the* COMMON MAN *and ringingly addresses the audience while the* COMMON MAN *watches from the rostrum*)

CROMWELL (*indicating the banners, etc*)   **Scene 8**
    What Englishman can behold without awe,
    The Canvas and the Rigging of the Law!

(*A fanfare is heard*)

    Forbidden here the galley-master's whip—
    Hearts of Oak, in the Law's Great Ship.

(*A fanfare is heard. The* COMMON MAN *starts to tip-toe discreetly off* R *with the clearing-pole*)

(*To the Common Man*) Where are you going?
    COMMON MAN. I've finished here, sir.
    CROMWELL. You're the Foreman of the Jury.
    COMMON MAN. Oh, no, sir.

(*The* COMMON MAN *exits down* R, *deposits the pole and re-enters*)

CROMWELL. You are John Dauncie. A general dealer.
COMMON MAN (*gloomily*) Yes.

CROMWELL. Foreman of the Jury.

(*The* COMMON MAN *crosses to the benches* L, *takes the first cap and puts it on*)

Does the cap fit?

COMMON MAN. Yes, sir.

CROMWELL.
So, now we'll apply the good, plain sailor's art,
And fix these quicksands on the Law's plain chart!

(*A fanfare is heard.* CROMWELL *moves to the table and takes a document from the portfolio.*

NORFOLK *and* CRANMER *enter* R *on the rostrum.* CRANMER *carries a Bible.* MORE *rises.* NORFOLK *sits in the throne chair* L *and* CRANMER *in the throne chair* R. *The* COMMON MAN *sits on the bench* L)

NORFOLK. Sir Thomas More, you are called before us here at the Hall of Westminster to answer charges of High Treason. Nevertheless, and though you have heinously offended the King's majesty, we hope that if you will even now forthink and repent of your obstinate opinions, you may still taste his gracious pardon.

MORE. My lords, I thank you. Howbeit, I make my petition to Almighty God that He will keep me in this my honest mind to the last hour that I shall live. As for the matters you charge me with, I fear, from my present weakness, that neither my wit nor my memory will serve to make sufficient answers. I should be glad to sit down.

NORFOLK. Be seated.

(MORE *sits in the chair* C)

Master Secretary Cromwell, are you ready?

CROMWELL. Yes, my lord. (*He moves to* R *of More*)

NORFOLK. Have you the charge?

CROMWELL. I have, my lord.

NORFOLK. Then read the charge.

CROMWELL (*reading from his document*) "That you did conspire traitorously and maliciously to deny and deprive our liege Lord Henry of his undoubted certain title, Supreme Head of the Church in England.

MORE. But I have never denied this title.

CROMWELL. You refused the oath tendered to you at the Tower and elsewhere.

MORE. Silence is not denial. And for my silence I am punished with imprisonment. Why have I been called again? (*At this point he is sensing that the trial has been in some way rigged*)

NORFOLK. On a charge of High Treason, Sir Thomas.

CROMWELL (*moving to the table*) For which the penalty is *not* imprisonment.

MORE. Death—comes for us all, my lords. Yes, even for Kings, he comes, to whom amidst all their royalty and brute strength he will neither kneel nor make them any reverence nor pleasantly desire them to come forth, but roughly grasp them by the very breast and rattle them until they be stark dead. So causing their bodies to be buried in a pit and sending *them* to judgement— whereof at their death their success is uncertain.

CROMWELL (*moving down LC and facing the "Jury"*) Treason enough here!

NORFOLK. The death of kings is not in question, Sir Thomas.

MORE. Nor mine, I trust, until I'm proven guilty.

NORFOLK (*leaning forward urgently*) Your life lies in your own hand, Thomas, as it always has.

MORE (*absorbing this*) For our own deaths, my lord, yours and mine, dare we for shame desire to enter the Kingdom with ease, when Our Lord Himself entered with so much pain?

(MORE *now faces* CROMWELL, *his eyes sparkling with suspicion; and the interchange goes ding-dong, a duelling scene*)

CROMWELL (*moving to L of More*) Now, Sir Thomas, you stand upon your silence.

MORE. I do.

CROMWELL (*turning to the "Jury"*) But, Gentlemen of the Jury, there are many kinds of silence. Consider first the silence of a man when he is dead. Let us say we go into the room where he is lying: and let us say it is the dead of night—there's nothing like darkness for sharpening the ear—and we listen. What do we hear? (*He listens intently*) Silence. What does it betoken, this silence? Nothing. This is silence pure and simple. But consider another case. Suppose I were to draw a dagger from my sleeve and make to kill the prisoner with it; and suppose their lordships there, instead of crying out for me to stop or crying out for help to stop me, maintained their silence. That would *betoken*. It would betoken a willingness that I should do it, and under the law they would be guilty with me. So silence can, according to the circumstances, speak. Consider now the circumstances of the prisoner's silence. The oath was put to good and faithful subjects up and down the country and they had declared His Grace's title to be just and good. And when it came to the prisoner, he refused. He calls this silence. Yet is there a man in this court, is there a man in this country, who does not *know* Sir Thomas More's opinion of this title? Of course not. But how can that be? Because this silence betokened—nay, this silence *was*—not silence at all, but most eloquent denial.

MORE (*with some of the academic's impatience for a shoddy line of reasoning*) Not so, Mr Secretary, the maxim is "*qui tacet consentire*". (*He turns to the Foreman*) The maxim of the law is—(*very carefully*) "Silence gives consent." If therefore, you wish to construe what my silence "betokened", you must construe that I consented, not that I denied.

CROMWELL. Is that what the world, in fact, construes from it? Do you pretend that is what you *wish* the world to construe from it?

MORE. The world must construe according to its wits. This court must construe according to the law.

CROMWELL (*crossing to* R *of the steps*) I put it to the court that the prisoner is perverting the law—making smoky what should be a clear light to discover to the court his own wrongdoing. (*His official indignation is slipping into genuine anger*)

MORE. The law is not a "light", for you or any man to see by; the law is not an instrument of any kind. (*To the Foreman*) The law is a causeway upon which so long as he keeps to it a citizen may walk safely. (*Earnestly*) In matters of conscience . . .

CROMWELL (*crossing to* R *of More; bitterly smiling*) The conscience, the conscience . . .

MORE (*turning to Cromwell*) The word is not familiar to you?

CROMWELL. By God, too familiar! I am very used to hear it in the mouths of criminals.

MORE. I am used to hear bad men misuse the name of God, yet God exists. (*He turns to the Foreman*) In matters of conscience, the loyal subject is more bounden to be loyal *to* his conscience than any other thing.

CROMWELL (*crossing to* L *of More; breathing hard*) And so provide a noble motive for his frivolous self-conceit.

MORE (*earnestly*) It is not so, Master Cromwell—very and pure necessity for respect of my own soul.

CROMWELL (*crossing to* L *of the steps*) Your own self, you mean.

MORE. Yes, a man's soul is his self.

(CROMWELL *moves to* R *of More and thrusts his face into* MORE'S. *They hate each other and each other's standpoint*)

CROMWELL. A miserable thing, whatever you call it, that lives like a bat in a Sunday School. A shrill, incessant pedagogue about your own salvation—but nothing to say of your place in the State! Under the King! In a great native country!

MORE (*not untouched*) Is it my place to say good to the State sickness? Can I help my King by giving him lies when he asks for truth? Will you help England by populating her with liars?

(CROMWELL *backs to the table, his face stiff with malevolence*)

CROMWELL. My lords, I wish to call—(*he raises his voice*) Sir Richard Rich.

(RICH *enters* L. *He is now splendidly official, in dress and bearing. Even* NORFOLK *is a little impressed*)

Sir Richard . . . (*He indicates Cranmer*)

(RICH *crosses and stands below the rostrum in front of Cranmer*)

CRANMER (*rising and proffering the Bible*) I do solemnly swear . . .

RICH. I do solemnly swear that the evidence I shall give before the court shall be the truth, the whole truth, and nothing but the truth.

CRANMER (*discreetly*) "So help me God," Sir Richard.

RICH. So help me, God.

(CRANMER *sits*)

NORFOLK (*pointing to* L *of the steps*) Take your stand there, Sir Richard.

(RICH *stands* L *of the steps*)

CROMWELL (*moving down* LC) Now, Rich, on the twelfth of March, you were at the Tower?

RICH. I was.

CROMWELL. With what purpose?

RICH. I was sent to carry away the prisoner's books.

CROMWELL. Did you talk with the prisoner?

RICH. Yes.

CROMWELL. Did you talk about the King's Supremacy of the Church?

RICH. Yes.

CROMWELL. What did you say?

RICH. I said to him: "Supposing there was an Act of Parliament to say that I, Richard Rich, were to be King, would not you, Master More, take me for King?" "That I would," he said, "for then you would be King."

CROMWELL. Yes?

RICH. Then he said . . .

NORFOLK (*sharply*) The prisoner?

RICH. Yes, my lord. "But I will put you a higher case," he said. "How if there were an Act of Parliament to say that God should not be God?"

MORE. This is true; and then you said . . .

NORFOLK. Silence! (*To Rich*) Continue.

RICH. I said, "Ah, but I will put you a middle case. Parliament has made our King Head of the Church. Why will you not accept him?"

NORFOLK (*strung up*) Well?

RICH. Then he said that Parliament had no power to do it.

NORFOLK. Repeat the prisoner's words.

RICH. He said, "Parliament has not the competence". Or words to that effect.

CROMWELL. He denied the title?

RICH. He did.

(*All but* RICH *look to* MORE, *but he looks at Rich*)

MORE. In good faith, Rich, I am sorrier for your perjury than my peril.

NORFOLK. Do you deny this?

MORE (*desperately*) Yes! My lords, if I were a man who heeded not the taking of an oath, you know well I need not to be here. Now I will take an oath. (*He rises*) If what Master Rich has said is true, then I pray I may never see God in the face. Which I would not say were it otherwise for anything on earth.

CROMWELL (*to the Foreman; calmly and technically*) That is not evidence.

MORE. Is it probable—is it probable—that after so long a silence, on this the very point so urgently sought of me, I should open my mind to such a man as that?

CROMWELL (*moving behind More's chair; to Rich*) Do you wish to modify your testimony?

RICH. No, Secretary.

MORE (*crossing to R and facing Norfolk and Cranmer*) There were two other men. Southwell and Palmer.

CROMWELL. Unhappily, Sir Richard Southwell and Master Palmer are both in Ireland on the King's business. (*He takes a document from the portfolio*)

(MORE *gestures helplessly*)

It has no bearing. I have their deposition here in which the court will see that they state that being busy with the prisoner's books they did not hear what was said. (*He hands the document to the Foreman*)

(*The* FOREMAN *examines the document with much seriousness*)

MORE. If I had really said this, is it not obvious he would instantly have called these men to witness?

CROMWELL. Sir Richard, have you anything to add?

RICH. Nothing, Mr Secretary.

NORFOLK. Sir Thomas?

MORE (*crossing to the chair C and looking at the Foreman*) To what purpose? (*He sits*) I am a dead man. (*To Cromwell*) You have your desire of me. What you have hunted me for is not my actions, but the thoughts of my heart. It is a long road you have opened. For first men will disclaim their hearts and presently they will have no hearts. God help the people whose statesmen walk your road.

NORFOLK. Then the witness may withdraw.

(RICH *moves down* R)

MORE. I *have* one question to ask the witness.

(RICH *stops*)

That's a chain of office you are wearing.

(RICH *reluctantly faces More*)

May I see it?

(NORFOLK *motions* RICH *to approach and he moves to More*)

(*He examines the medallion*) The red dragon. (*To Cromwell*) What's this?

CROMWELL. Sir Richard is appointed Attorney General for Wales.

MORE (*looking into Rich's face; with pain and amusement*) For Wales? Why, Richard, it profits a man nothing to give his soul for the whole world—but for Wales . . . !

(RICH, *stiff-faced, but infrangibly dignified, exits down* R)

CROMWELL. Now I must ask the court's indulgence. I have a message for the prisoner from the King. (*He moves to* L *of More. Urgently*) Sir Thomas, I am empowered to tell you that even now . . .

MORE. No, no. It cannot be.

CROMWELL (*moving to the table*) The case rests.

(NORFOLK *stares at More*)

(*To Norfolk*) My lord!

NORFOLK (*taking refuge in a rigorously official tone*) The Jury will retire and consider the evidence.

(*The* FOREMAN *rises*)

CROMWELL (*moving to the Foreman*) Considering the evidence, it shouldn't be necessary for them to retire. (*He stands over the Foreman*) Is it necessary?

(*The* FOREMAN *shakes his head*)

NORFOLK. Then is the prisoner guilty or not guilty?

FOREMAN. Guilty, my lord.

(NORFOLK *and* CRANMER *rise*. CROMWELL *moves to the table*)

NORFOLK. Prisoner at the bar, you have been found guilty of High Treason. The sentence of the court . . .

MORE. My lord!

(NORFOLK *breaks off*)

(*He has a sly smile. From this point to the end of the Play, his manner is of one who has fulfilled all his obligations and will now consult no interests but his own*) My lord, when *I* was practising the law, the manner was to ask the prisoner *before* pronouncing sentence, if he had anything to say.

NORFOLK (*flummoxed*) Have you anything to say?

MORE (*rising*) Yes.

(NORFOLK, CRANMER *and the* FOREMAN *resume their seats*)

To avoid this I have taken every path my winding wits could find. Now that the court has determined to condemn me, God knoweth how, I will discharge my mind—concerning my indictment and the King's title. The indictment is grounded in an Act of Parliament which is directly repugnant to the Law of God. The King in Parliament cannot bestow the Supremacy of the Church because it is a Spiritual Supremacy. And more to this, the immunity of the Church is promised both in Magna Carta and the King's own Coronation Oath.

CROMWELL (*moving* L) Now we plainly see that you *are* malicious!

MORE. Not so, Mr Secretary. (*He pauses then launches, very quietly and ruminatively into his final stocktaking*) I am the King's true subject and pray for him and all the realm. I do none harm, I say none harm, I think none harm. And if this be not enough to keep a man alive, in good faith I long not to live. I have, since I came into prison, been several times in such a case that I thought to die within the hour, and I thank Our Lord I was never sorry for it, but rather sorry when it passed. And therefore, my poor body is at the King's pleasure. Would God my death might do him some good. (*With a great flash of scorn and anger*) Nevertheless, it is not for the Supremacy that you have sought my blood—but because I would not bend to the marriage.

(NORFOLK, CRANMER *and the* FOREMAN *rise. During the reading of the sentence by* NORFOLK, *the Scene is changed*)

NORFOLK. Prisoner at the bar, you have been found guilty of the charge of High Treason.

(*The murmuring and noises of a large crowd is heard off. It is formalized almost into a chant and mounting so that* NORFOLK *has to shout the end of his speech. The Coats of Arms are raised*)

The sentence of the Court is that you shall be taken from this court to the Tower, thence to the place of execution, and there your head shall be stricken from your body...

(*The* LIGHTS *fade, leaving three pools of light,* L, R *and at the top of the stairway. A black cut-cloth is lowered behind the stairway. The* COMMON MAN *removes his hat, puts it on its pole and pushes the benches off* L. CROMWELL *pushes the table off* L. *The* COMMON MAN *pushes the chair off* L. CROMWELL *drags the property basket up* C *and takes a Headsman's mask from it. He puts it on the* COMMON MAN *who goes up the stairway, lifts up a trap so that it becomes the block, gets an axe from behind the screen and stands* L *of the block.*
CROMWELL *pushes the basket off and exits with it* L. *The lights on the cyclorama come slowly up, so that the Headsman with the axe and block are silhouetted against a light of steadily increasing brilliance*)

—and may God have mercy on your soul.

(NORFOLK *and* CRANMER *take the throne chairs off* R.
NORFOLK *re-enters carrying a wine cup and stands* LC *of the rostrum.*
MORE *moves down* L.
CRANMER *re-enters and stands* C *of the rostrum.*
The WOMAN *enters up* R, *crosses and stands up* L. *When the stage
is set, the crowd noises stop and all movement ceases except for* MORE *who
moves up* C)   **Scene 9**

I can come no further, Thomas. (*He proffers the wine cup*) Here, drink
this.
    MORE. My Master had easel and gall, not wine, given Him to
drink. Let me be going.

    (NORFOLK *crosses down* L.
        MARGARET *runs on* R *on the rostrum*)

    MARGARET. Father! (*She runs to More 'and flings herself upon him*)
Father! Father, Father, Father, Father!
    MORE. Have patience, Margaret, and trouble not thyself. Death
comes for us all; even at our birth—even at our birth death does
but stand aside a little and every day he looks towards us and muses
somewhat whether that day or the next he will draw nigh. It is the
course of nature and the will of God. You have long known the
secrets of my heart.

    (MARGARET *disengages herself, crosses and exits down* L.
        NORFOLK *follows her off.* MORE *moves down* C. CRANMER *moves
to the foot of the steps*)

    WOMAN (*moving down* L) Sir Thomas!

    (MORE *stops*)

Remember me, Sir Thomas? When you were Chancellor, you gave
a false judgement against me. Remember that now.
    MORE. Woman, you see how I am occupied. (*With sudden decision
he moves to* R *of her. Crisply*) I remember your matter well, and if I
had to give sentence now I assure you I should not alter it. You have
no injury; so go your ways; and content yourself; and trouble me
not.

    (*The* WOMAN *exits down* L)

(*He turns and moves swiftly to the steps, then stops as he sees Cranmer.
Quite kindly*) I beseech Your Grace, go back.

    (CRANMER, *offended, moves down* R. *The pools of light fade. The lights
on the cyclorama are now dazzlingly brilliant*)

(*He goes up the stairway. To the Headsman*) Friend, be not afraid of
your office. You send me to God.
    CRANMER (*envious rather than waspish*) You're very sure of that, Sir
Thomas.

(CRANMER *exits down* R. MORE *removes his hat, revealing the grey disordered hair*)

MORE. He will not refuse one who is so blithe to go to Him. (*He kneels at the block*)

(*Immediately there is a harsh roar of kettle-drums and the* LIGHTS BLACK-OUT. *The drums cease.*

MORE *exits in the* BLACK-OUT. *The* HEADSMAN *removes his mask*)

HEADSMAN (*from the darkness*) Behold—the head—of a traitor.

(*The* LIGHTS *come up. The* COMMON MAN *descends the stairway and stands* C)

COMMON MAN (*to the audience*) I'm breathing. Are you breathing, too? It's nice, isn't it? It isn't difficult to keep alive, friends—just don't *make* trouble—or if you must make trouble, make the sort of trouble that's expected. Well, I don't need to tell you that. Good night, friends. If we should bump into one another, recognize me.

The COMMON MAN *exits* L *as—*

the CURTAIN *falls*

The main purpose of the Play being to celebrate the man; its essential action accords with the facts.

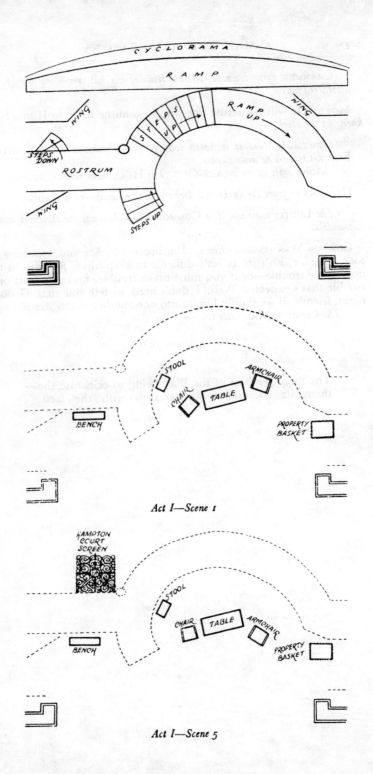

Act I—Scene 1

Act I—Scene 5

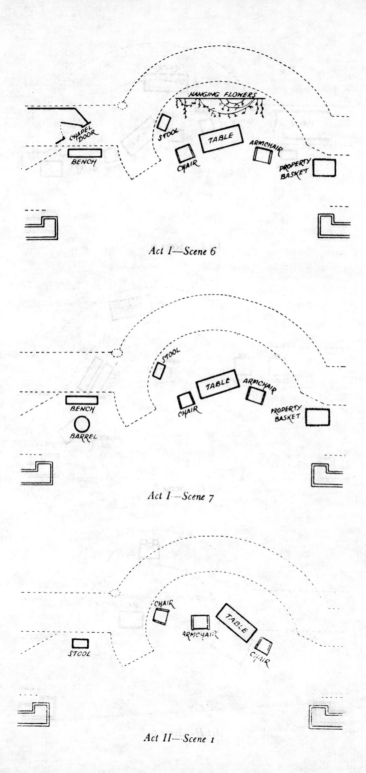

Act I—Scene 6

Act I—Scene 7

Act II—Scene 1

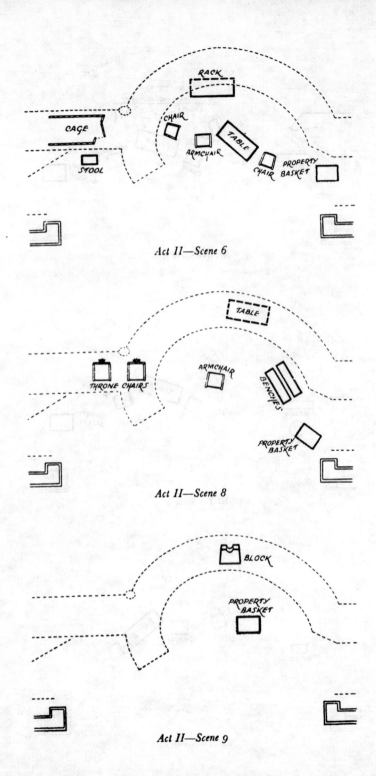

Act II—Scene 6

Act II—Scene 8

Act II—Scene 9

Any character costumes and wigs needed in the performance of this plays can be obtained from Charles H Fox Ltd, 25 Shelton Street, London, W.C.2

FURNITURE AND PROPERTY LIST

ACT I

On stage: Table (C) *On it:* white linen cloth. velour cloth. white linen cloth
Large armchair (L of table)
Small chair (R of table)
Short bench (below rostrum R)
Stool (in curve of stairway RC)
Property basket. *In it:* Steward's coat and cap; wicker tray with a pewter jug of wine, a silver cup, 5 goblets, brass inkwell, 2 quills, Wolsey's portfolio with papers and documents, More's slippers, pair of spectacles. book

Off stage: Letter (STEWARD)
Brass candlestick (WOLSEY)
Brass candlestick (MORE)
Oar, boatman's coat and hat *(in flies)*
Mug (MARGARET)
Red robe and Cardinal's hat *(in flies)*
Property basket (R) *In it:* publican's hat, apron with duster and matches in pocket, 2 horn mugs (COMMON MAN)
Barrel (COMMON MAN)
Lighted candle in candlestick (COMMON MAN)
Inn sign (COMMON MAN)
Wine bottle (CROMWELL)

Personal: CROMWELL: coins
STEWARD: cross
CHAPUYS: small ebony cross, coin
RICH: coin
HENRY: pilot's whistle, dagger

ACT II

Strike :   Barrel, candlestick, wine bottle
        2 mugs
        Inn sign
        Bench down R

Set :   Table (angled I C) *On it :* velour and linen cloths
      Armchair (C)
      Small chair (L of table)
      Small chair (L of rostrum)
      Stool under stairway

Off stage :   Book (COMMON MAN)
      Shelf with books, globe of world, handbell, hour-glass, etc. (*in flies*)
      Portfolio. *In it :* documents (CROMWELL)
      Letter (CHAPUYS)
      Bundle of bracken (MARGARET)
      Sickle (ROPER)
      Portfolio (RICH)
      Small book (RICH)
      Pewter inkwell (RICH)
      Quill pen (RICH)
      Property basket. *In it :* jailer's skull-cap and coat, portfolio, headsman's mask (COMMON MAN)
      Letter (*in flies*)
      Document (CROMWELL)
      Basket. *In it :* napkin, cheese, custard pie (MARGARET)
      Bottle of wine (ROPER)
      Clearing-pole (CROMWELL)
      2 benches with poles (COMMON MAN)
      2 throne chairs (COMMON MAN)
      Bible (CRANMER)
      Axe (COMMON MAN)
      Wine cup (NORFOLK)

Personal :   COMMON MAN: spectacles
      ROPER: cross
      MORE: chain of office
      RICH: chain of office

LIGHTING PLOT

Property fittings required: 2 brass candlesticks, 1 pewter candlestick

ACT I

To open: The stage in darkness

Cue 1   After rise of CURTAIN   (Page 1)
Snap in spot focused vertically on the COMMON MAN *seated on basket down* L

Cue 2   COMMON MAN: "Matthew!"   (Page 1)
Bring up general lighting quickly

Cue 3   STEWARD: ". . . out of practice."   (Page 9)
Cross fade lights for Scene 2

Cue 4   WOLSEY exits with candle   (Page 13)
Fade general lighting
Bring in spot on COMMON MAN
Bring in ripple effect on cyclorama

Cue 5   MORE (*off*) "Boat! Boat!"   (Page 13)
Bring up lights for riverside Scene 3

Cue 6   MORE exits R   (Page 15)
Fade front lighting and ripple effect

Cue 7   STEWARD: "Home again."   (Page 15)
Bring up general lighting. Fade Common Man spot

Cue 8   MORE and MARGARET exit   (Page 19)
Dim to BLACK-OUT
Bring up spot for Cloak RC

Cue 9   Follows above cue   (Page 19)
Bring up Common Man spot

Cue 10   COMMON MAN: "Whether we follow . . ."   (Page 19)
Fade Cloak spot

Cue 11   COMMON MAN exits   (Page 19)
Bring up lighting for Hampton Court Scene
Fade Common Man spot

Cue 12   COMMON MAN: ". . . in a fortnight."   (Page 23)
Lights change for Garden Scene

Cue 13   MORE and ROPER exit   (Page 38)
Lights change for Inn Scene

ACT II

To open: General lighting for More's house

Cue 14   COMMON MAN: "... fell for it."   (Page 53)
             Lights change for Scene 2

Cue 15   STEWARD: "Sir Thomas More's again."   (Page 57)
             Lights change so that the setting looks drab and chilly

Cue 16   MORE: "When?"   (Page 60)
             Dim general lighting, leaving MORE *in pool of light* C

Cue 17   MORE: "... the merest plumber."   (Page 61)
             Lights change for Scene 4

Cue 18   CROMWELL: "And it's ravenous."   (Page 64)
             Cross fade lights to riverside effect

Cue 19   MARGARET, MORE *and* ROPER *exit* R   (Page 68)
             Cross fade lights for prison night scene

Cue 20   CROMWELL *and* RICH *exit* L   (Page 74)
             Lights change from night to cold grey morning light

Cue 21   MORE: "... plain, simple men."   (Page 80)
             Cross fade lights for Trial Scene

Cue 22   NORFOLK: "... from your body ..."   (Page 87)
             Fade lights leaving 3 pools of light L, R *and at the top of the
                  stairway*

Cue 23   Follows above cue   (Page 87)
             Bring up lights on cyclorama

Cue 24   MORE *kneels*   (Page 89)
             BLACK-OUT

Cue 25   HEADSMAN: "... of a traitor."   (Page 89)
             Bring up general lighting

EFFECTS PLOT

ACT I

Cue 16	MORE: "How so, Your Grace?" *The music fades*	(Page 28)
Cue 17	MORE: ". . . overwhelms me." *Bells chime eight*	(Page 32)

ACT II

Cue 18	Before rise of CURTAIN *Ringing of loud single bell*	(Page 44)
Cue 19	After rise of CURTAIN *Stop bell*	(Page 44)
Cue 20	ALICE: "Be off at once." *Bell strikes seven*	(Page 79)
Cue 21	MORE: ". . . plain, simple men." *Fanfare*	(Page 80)
Cue 22	CROMWELL: ". . . of the Law!" *Fanfare*	(Page 80)
Cue 23	CROMWELL: ". . . Law's Great Ship!" *Fanfare*	(Page 80)
Cue 24	CROMWELL: ". . . Law's plain chart!" *Fanfare*	(Page 81)
Cue 25	NORFOLK: ". . . of High Treason." *Murmuring and noises of a large crowd*	(Page 87)
Cue 26	The WOMAN enters R *Crowd noises cease*	(Page 88)
Cue 27	MORE kneels *Harsh roar of kettle-drums*	(Page 89)

MADE AND PRINTED IN GREAT BRITAIN BY
LATIMER TREND & COMPANY LTD PLYMOUTH

MADE IN ENGLAND